ETHICAL DILEMMAS IN LIBRARIES

A Collection of Case Studies

ETHICAL DILEMMAS IN LIBRARIES

A Collection of Case Studies

HERBERT S. WHITE

Distinguished Professor
School of Library and Information Science
Indiana University

G. K. HALL & CO.
New York
MAXWELL MACMILLAN CANADA
Toronto
MAXWELL MACMILLAN INTERNATIONAL
New York Oxford Singapore Sydney

G. K. Hall & Co.
Macmillan Publishing Company
866 Third Avenue
New York, NY 10022

Maxwell Macmillan Canada, Inc.
1200 Eglinton Avenue East, Suite 200
Don Mills, Ontario M3C 3N1

Macmillan Publishing Company is part of the Maxwell Communication Group of Companies.

Library of Congress Catalog Card Number: 91-47495

Printed in the United States of America

printing number
1 2 3 4 5 6 7 8 9 10

Library of Congress Cataloging-in-Publication Data

White, Herbert S.
Ethical dilemmas in libraries : a collection of case studies / Herbert S. White.
p. cm.
ISBN 0-8161-1972-4 (hc) ISBN 0-8161-1973-2 (pb)
1. Library personnel management—Moral and ethical aspects—Case studies. 2. Librarians—Professional ethics—Case studies.
I. Title.
Z682.W649 1992
023′.9—dc20 91-47495
CIP

The paper used in this publication meets the minimum requirements of American National Standard for Information Sciences—Permanence of Paper for Printed Library materials. ANSI Z39.48-1984. ♾™

Dedicated to my wife,
Virginia,
whose insights and common sense have been invaluable
to me throughout my management career.

Contents

Introduction

The use of case studies is a time-honored and traditional approach in the teaching of management. Its purpose is to stimulate in the classroom the kinds of issues that could arise in a real managerial setting, where decisions have to be made. Case studies provide, in addition to the theories and concepts of management invariably covered in lectures and readings, an opportunity to practice, and to learn through experience and, if necessary, by making mistakes. The case study in the teaching of management is the equivalent of the laboratory experiment in the teaching of chemistry or of batting practice in preparation for playing a baseball game.

It is therefore essential that case studies simulate, as far as possible, the kinds of issues that will confront the manager in what is called "the real world." Managers are called upon to make decisions; indeed it is the primary requirement of management either to make decisions directly or see to it that decisions are made by others. Good decisions are better than bad ones, but in many instances even a bad decision is preferable to no decision. Management theorists have explained that the absence of a decision is in itself a decision, because a refusal to decide clearly sends a message of paralysis or indifference to those awaiting a resolution of an issue. Individuals who are paralyzed by the decision process cannot manage, but it is clearly to everyone's advantage that more good decisions than bad decisions be made.

What represents a good decision? To some extent we know only after the fact, and even then there can be only the perceptions of the manager making the judgment and of those who are affected by it. Decisions affect both policies and people, and these include the manager who makes the decision, the subordinates who are involved directly or indirectly, the levels of management above the deciding manager, the library clients and customers, and even those affected on an affiliated basis (vendors, the personnel department, the university or city attorney, etc.). It can be seen that every decision affects many individuals, and their perceptions of the "rightness" of any given decision will vary. And yet decisions must be made, because the dynamics of organization suggest that while not all change is good all good comes from change, and also that a problem that is ignored only gets worse.

It has been suggested, and it has certainly been my observation in the twenty-five years of operational management experience that preceded my role as a teacher, that management responsibilities inhibit an individual manager's freedom and options. That is contrary to the perception of management created in TV situation comedies; however, those of us who have managed recognize that although the management relationships depicted on television may be humorous, they have little relationship to reality. The danger is that individuals influenced by "learning" from television will believe that what is depicted as management issues on these programs represents reality. It does not. In the real world, managers have very little freedom and far less flexibility than they would like to have. Some of this is caused by organizational rules, by laws and regulations, and by the threat of litigation. However, the greatest part is caused by the realization that managers are ultimately responsible for seeing that their decisions work for the organization whose interests they are charged to represent. This then leads me immediately to the first ground rule to be applied to the consideration of options in case studies: Does the solution work for the library? If it does, then perhaps unhappiness on the part of individuals may just have to be endured, although we have to assess the potential impact of that as well. If the solution does not work for the organization, then the fact that particular individuals are deliriously happy is really irrelevant. Solutions that don't work for the library are not acceptable solutions, regardless of for whom else they work.

The impacts of management decisions can therefore be seen as far-reaching. Such decisions not only have direct and immediate effects on individuals inside and outside the library, they can have delayed effects far into the future. They establish precedents for future actions and future decisions. In the glaring light of hindsight, they can be second-guessed and shown to have been wrong. It is little wonder that some individuals charged with making decisions avoid making them for as long as possible. They stall, they refuse to read their mail, they fail to return phone calls, they argue that they need more time even when they have no plans with regard to how to use this time, they appoint committees not because there is any need to do so but because it is a convenient and cosmetic device for avoiding the responsibility of making decisions.

All of these tactics are well understood and well documented. Indeed, the term "bureaucrat" when used derisively, is usually intended to mean a person who refuses to make decisions based on the merits of an issue but allows existing policies and precedents—even when never intended for that purpose (nobody ever consciously urged a manager to make a bad decision)—to make decisions for him or her. Such decisions are made not because they will be better, but because no blame will result from them. Bureaucrats may make bad decisions, but that does not matter to them if the decisions are safe for them personally. Even more frequently they make no decisions at all; that is even safer.

The reasons for decision-avoidance in any setting, and I am still not talking specifically about libraries, are easy to understand. Yet it is clear that managers are appointed precisely because they are expected to make decisions. Not all decisions are difficult. Some are absurdly easy, either because they are dictated by common sense or because it is clear that what we would like to do and what we ought to do converge into a single main stream. There are fortunately many such decisions, or we would all suffer constant stress; but these are not the issues worth talking about in management case studies. The use of such examples trivializes the whole process. I can recall an absurd case study from my own training as an industrial manager. In this case, a subordinate has just received a telephone message that his daughter has been involved in an automobile accident and is in the hospital in critical condition. Should you allow him to leave early to go to the hospital? Of course you should! Even if you do not have a compassionate bone in your body, you recognize that if you fail to let him leave not only will he do no useful work for the rest of the day, but his anxiety will distract and undermine the work of all of the others. This is a case study in which all of the factors lead to the same obvious conclusion. There are such instances, but they are not worth writing about or talking about in a classroom setting.

Management does consist to a great extent of applications of common sense and the practice of the golden rule. Almost any student should be able to participate at that level. What makes management decisions complex and difficult is that frequently decisions can have both positive and negative effects, and—more important—that individuals differ in their outlooks, their value systems, and their reactions to issues. This comes as a great surprise to some students when they begin discussing case studies in the classroom setting. They find that what is "obvious" to them is not at all obvious to other students, and there can be strong disagreements as to what should be done. Since in the real management world they will be dealing with individuals (as subordinates, superiors, and clients) who may react just as unexpectedly and just as differently as do their fellow students, the purpose of presenting these cases is to familiarize the learner with complex issues that are subject to multiple reactions and interpretations. In each case there are inevitably several points of view and several options to be considered. One purpose of case study analysis is to examine what brought the subjects to this impasse and how it *might* have been avoided; "*could* have been avoided" is too strong a phrase because some problems, like Greek tragedy, are truly unavoidable. The other purpose is to determine what should now be done, in the face of the reality that confronts us.

The great danger in this process is that the student will consider the solution "obvious." Obvious for whom? For the student and his or her own value system? Isn't that value system irrelevant for those who do not share the same perception, and isn't this difference precisely what we need to concern ourselves about? The analysis of case studies is based on a careful and minute identification and evaluation of options that emerge as both possible and plausible. The oft-cited and obviously helpful golden rule then needs to be restated. It is no longer "Do unto others as you would have them do unto you." It is rather, insofar as possible, "Do unto others as those others would prefer that you do unto them." What you would have them do unto you may not matter! Perhaps you yearn for promotion, recognition, and participation, but they don't. They may want a job that provides routine and security, and that allows them to concentrate on outside hobbies or home responsibilities. It is not impossible that a board chairman is more concerned about the library's budget than the quality of library service. How should we deal with such people, who are not as we would prefer them to be?

We must reach individuals on their own basis of communication, but at the same time our responsibilities as managers remind us that the solution must work or nothing else matters. If I criticize a subordinate and that person resigns as a result, is that a problem? Not if that was the hoped-for result; but certainly, if the resignation produces panic in the manager because it will have catastrophic organizational or even personal consequences, it *is* a problem. What happens if a grievance is filed instead? Have we anticipated all of these possibilities before voicing the criticism? If the criticized subordinate pulls out a gun and shoots the supervisor, then this reaction was not only unanticipated but also tragic. That is something all students can understand.

Management is complex because other people are different from us. It is here that the teaching of management to librarians and future librarians takes on an additional dimension to that offered in business schools. Library science students are frequently reluctant to become managers. They were not drawn to this profession by the desire to achieve power over others, and many are genuinely surprised to learn that issues of management have anything to do with their chosen profession. Another difference is that many students come to our classes with a highly developed sense of social awareness and social purpose. That is obviously commendable, but it can get in the way of the analytical process when we begin by already knowing what is "right" and what is "moral," because those definitions vary with the perceptions of the individual. Thus right and moral become very subjective definitions, and "do the right thing" can be, in a management setting, not only a dangerous guideline but absolute gibberish. Library educators are often urged to impress moral and ethical concepts on their students. By and large in our field this is unnecessary, as it might indeed be very necessary in other fields. Instead our students need to understand, particularly as librarians but in any case as managers, that the issue of ethics and morality is indeed important but is defined differently by various individuals. None of these views can be dismissed outright in a management setting without disastrous results. Telling someone he or she is unethical or immoral is almost never a useful approach, quite aside from the fact that it is also arrogant. My role in the classroom, when I encounter such thinking, is to serve as devil's advocate. I challenge all opinions and "credos," as indeed others in any real-case analyses would challenge them. Decisions based on such a subjective framework can exhibit very dangerous tunnel vision.

There are, however, two generalizations that I have found to apply quite consistently. The first is that students, very much unlike the practitioners they will shortly become, have no qualms about making decisions in a case-study setting. Indeed, they will make them quickly and confidently based on incomplete information, on contradictory information, and sometimes on no information whatsoever. Students tend to be an impatient and sometimes, in this setting, a reckless lot. Caution comes later, with the first job.

The second generalization is that the more committed, the more articulate, the more persuasive, and the more passionate in commitment the student is, the more difficulty he or she may have with the management course and the case study approach. The students' desire is to solve, to fix, and to apply the conclusions with which they came to the classroom and to the university. In a world in which everyone were exactly alike that might be appropriate, but there is no such world, not even for librarians. The process of making the case study solutions fit the conclusions with which they began is something engineers call retrofitting; but finding facts and ignoring others, and making assumptions without labeling them as assumptions, is a very dangerous process in management. It is often the most articulate and most assertive students who have difficulty with case studies. So do students who are simply used to memorizing what they have been told. Such students are looking for "the" answer, and they want the instructor to tell them what that is so they can write it down and spew it back on tests. Some of these students get high grades in other courses simply through hard effort and memorization, but in library management case analyses it is the process of analysis that matters, and not the specific conclusion reached. The conclusion is not the key issue as long as the student has examined all of the alternatives and evaluated the likely reactions to the conclusion ultimately chosen. Whether that conclusion turned out to be "correct" is something a classroom setting cannot and need not determine. We can, at best, deal in probabilities, and in increasing the odds for success. This is not an exact process with a specific answer. It is not a matter of applying specific rules to material to be cataloged.

If the individuals in case studies all differ, are there any generalizations that tend to apply at least to most of them? There are, but these are highly personalized; and in case study analysis we must concentrate not on what *we* think, but on what others think or might think, and on what might prompt their behavior. We already know what we think. That is the easy part. But what thoughts do most other people share? They think that they are nice and decent people who don't ever consciously hurt others. They think they are fair and they think they are reasonable, and consider themselves more fair and reasonable than others with whom they come into contact, including you as the manager. Finally, they will, as we all will, retrofit. Even students already know how to retrofit and to rationalize. In their initial approaches to case studies, students will come up with ideas that fit their conclusions and their convenience, and either hope for the best or fail to see the potential problems. It takes several weeks of case study exercises for students to understand that the issue is more complex than first appears, because they have forgotten that people are complex and not necessarily like themselves. If the solution seems "obvious," I urge students to dig some more because they have probably missed a great deal. The more they miss as managers, the greater the risk that the solution ultimately selected will not work as they thought it would—and in the final analysis, whether it works for the library is what matters.

This book of case studies follows in the tradition of a number of excellent case study textbooks in the library science field. Among our earlier and best writers on this topic are Mildred Lowell and Kenneth Shaffer. I have read and used their case studies, and I have borrowed some of their scenarios in creating my more modern settings. I acknowledge my debt to both of them.

In addition, both A. J. Anderson and Bruce Shuman write current-setting case studies. Anderson writes regularly for *Library Journal*, and as an admirer of his approach I become frustrated by the fact that publication space limitations allow the reactors only the opportunity to solve problems, and rarely to analyze alternatives. As I read these solutions I recognize that many of the potential issues have been missed, and I am certain that Anderson feels just as frustrated. Shuman tends to write within the fixed setting of a particular library. This provides continuity and a level of interest because one comes to know his people, but it also introduces a limitation because it is dangerous to apply his case studies directly to one's own settings. Shuman's people are not anyone else's people. That is why, as a teacher of management, I am constantly writing additional case studies to illustrate particular issues, and that is why I have written this book. Many of the case studies are drawn from personal experience and observation, and they are real. Only the names and places have been changed, and any similarity to real people and places is completely coincidental. Other case studies represent the development of a scenario that, although I have not heard it has happened, *may* have happened, or might happen tomorrow.

Case studies should be taught primarily as *exercises in analysis and only secondarily as exercises in solution* because it is the technique and not the conclusion that really matters. That is true because no matter how many case studies we give students to learn from, their first real experience on the job will expose them to something different. There will then be nothing in their specific recollection of what they did, or what the instructor said to do, to help them with this problem. We do not learn by solving case studies, because there are as many case studies as snowflakes. We learn by acquiring skills in analysis, in the identification of alternatives, and in the assessment of potential risks. It is particularly essential that library science students master this approach, because librarians have no grace period. They usually become managers or supervisors immediately upon graduation, and they will encounter situations that may have some similarities to what they have seen before but that are nevertheless unique. Because I teach management, I should be forgiven the belief that it is the most important course taught in library school. I consider it more important than, for example, reference work or collection development because, crucial as these skills are, without the management ability to create the appropriate setting one will not be in a position to do much in the way of either reference work or collection development. Good management creates an environment in which other good things are possible. This is what I believe and what I teach.

The suggested approach to these case studies, either for the student or for the librarian seeking to develop or hone skills, includes the following step-by-step approach: (1) What are the issues, problems and concerns that this case study presents? What are the individual concerns for the various protagonists mentioned? What are the issues for the library or its parent organization? (2) Could this problem have been avoided? If so, how? (3) In dealing with the present scenario, what are *all* of the options you can see? What are the benefits, shortcomings, and risks of applying any of these options? What is likely to happen? What *could* happen in the worst-case scenario? What then? (4) Which option have you decided to implement? Why this one rather than the others? What do you see as the likely consequences and how will you deal with them? (5) As a result of what you have decided to do, what is the impact on the library, or at least that part of it you are charged with managing?

The case studies as written provide no solutions, because finding a solution is the final and not the beginning process. Frequently, they are written from the standpoint of one of the protagonists, and the individual analyzing the case study must recognize that this immediately introduces a bias. All stories are presented from a specific point of view, and this includes case studies; they could all be written at least twice to read quite differently each time. At the end of the book I have included, for each case study, at least some of the issues that in my judgment need to be addressed. Individuals undertaking a written analysis should hold off looking at this section until they have completed what they consider a thorough analysis. Teachers who plan to assign these case studies for class discussion may prefer, to facilitate and speed the process, to refer to this section almost immediately. However, in my opinion the process of learning by trying and, if necessary, failing is the most important element. If we don't allow people to make mistakes in this abstract setting, we run the risk that they will make more serious errors when they are dealing with real people in real settings. They will make mistakes in any case, because good managers make more mistakes than bad ones. However, they also make far more good decisions than bad managers—and the worst managers are completely paralyzed by the decision-making process.

It was my original intent to divide this book into perhaps fourteen or fifteen sections, each representing a particular type of issue or problem, but I have been unable to follow that categorization. Case studies tend to be multifaceted, and they fit into more than one place. I have finally divided these case studies into only three groupings: those that deal primarily with management issues in interacting with subordinates; those that deal primarily with management issues in interacting with superiors; and those that deal with clients and patrons, although some management writers prefer the term *customers* to make the relationship more direct. There are similarities in all of the approaches, because all of the individuals with whom we interact will look at what we do in terms of their own perceived ultimate benefit. Therefore, even these three simple categorizations can sometimes become arbitrary.

I close this introduction with a grateful appreciation and recognition of the thousands of librarians and students who have been the creative influence in the generating of these case studies. As we learn quickly in management, and as I learned over and over in twenty-five years of operational management and then fifteen years of teaching and consulting, truth is certainly stranger than fiction. It is not necessary to invent farfetched scenarios. They have almost certainly already occurred somewhere, and if not, they will occur in your own libraries today or at the latest, tomorrow.

ETHICAL DILEMMAS IN LIBRARIES

A Collection of Case Studies

I

INTERACTIONS WITH SUBORDINATES

1

THE "HONOR" OF BEING A CLERK IN THE LIBRARY

The Murchison Plains Public Library, like the rest of the Murchison Plains municipal government, did not have a union. The southwestern part of the United States, unlike New England, rarely has municipal employee unions. It did have a civil service, and nonprofessional positions were categorized as Clerk I to Clerk VI level, each with general job descriptions and pay ranges. Murchison Plains usually hired its clerks at the starting end of the salary grid, and they then moved through the range based on annual increments voted by the city council. There were no merit increases as such, only the possibility of promotion or reclassification. Professional librarians were treated differently, and more in accordance with accountants and restaurant health inspectors. Their pay scales were also poor, but there was more flexibility, particularly in the ability to be hired above the low end of the range.

Although clerical levels up to VI existed within the city government, the library only had access to levels I through III. This was based on an evaluation performed about ten years ago, before Francine Schneider had become library director. She had been unable to find any paperwork to justify the levels decided upon, but the city's personnel office had made it very clear to her last year that it had no interest in reopening any of these discussions, lest it be forced to reexamine and perhaps upgrade clerical levels for agencies much larger than the library. Murchison Plains had no interest in paying more for municipal services than absolutely necessary, for the community was fiscally as well as politically conservative. Although the library had been reasonably well supported, at least compared to other public libraries in the region, Francine, who had grown up in that area of the country, understood that it would not be appreciated if she made waves.

While the public library did not have a union, it did have a staff association for all its nonprofessional employees, with elected officers. The association concentrated primarily on social functions such as picnics, the library bowling team, and bridal and baby showers as appropriate. Betsy Van Meter was president of the association. A younger employee who was both personable and articulate, Betsy was a natural leader, and if she had more education or for that matter more ambition she might have aspired to being a librarian. She had been with the Murchison Plains Library for six years, was a Clerk II in circulation services, and was from a large and well-known family. Francine dealt with her only occasionally, usually in the planning of the various social activities, and she liked Betsy very much. She assumed that when Betsy had asked to see her this morning, it concerned the planning of another social event. Perhaps it was time for the annual bowling dinner, at which Francine was usually asked to make the presentations.

She was wrong. The tone of the meeting was not menacing, but the subject was serious. Betsy said that she and some of the others had been talking about issues that had bothered them for some time, and they had agreed that these issues should be brought to Ms. Schneider's attention. They all realized that salaries at Murchison Plains were low and salary increases small. They had known that when they took their jobs, and they also knew there wasn't much that could be done about it except maybe move to Dallas or Tulsa. However, even within the Murchison Plains structure there were some differences that seemed just plain unfair, and there were two in particular they wanted to mention. They knew that there were clerks in municipal offices, such as the tax assessment office, who were rated at levels IV and V although their responsibilities were not any more complicated then those of clerks in the library. In addition, other municipal employees worked regular nine-to-five workdays with no evening hours or weekends. When some of the offices had occasional work at busy times in the evenings and on weekends, they received additional pay for working those unattractive hours. Library clerks, by contrast, regularly worked both evenings and weekends, without any change in their hourly rates. In fact they were just normally scheduled to work on Saturdays and Sundays as if they were any other days. When the library had changed its hours to open later in the morning and stay open until nine at night and increased the hours for both Saturday and Sunday, it simply meant that everybody had to work more hours at these unpopular times. The scheduling was fair, but this just meant that all of them had to suffer. They got to spend less time with their friends and families, and they didn't even get paid extra for it.

Francine knew that all of this was true, and her only rationale was that it had always been true. She also knew that the library did not have the funds to pay for reclassifications or for shift differentials for weekend or evening work, even in the unlikely event that the municipal controller's office were to agree even to the principle. Then, if the rates of pay were increased but the funds not allocated, it would mean that the library would have to curtail its hours, particularly in the evenings and on the weekends. That, of course, was when the library was busiest.

2

THE ENTHUSIASTIC HIGH-PRICED FILE CLERK

Edward Krikorian had now been library director at State University for three months, and the pieces were beginning to fall into place. It was his nature to move slowly and methodically, and to set the stage for what he thought might be difficult discussions. This was such an occasion; at least it might turn out to be.

He had invited Florence Van Horne, assistant director for technical services, to join him for an afternoon cup of coffee in his office. He had simply made the offer as he passed Florence's open door on the way to his own office. "Best offer I've had today," Florence had responded cheerfully. Now they were seated in the comfortable chairs that graced the director's office, and Edward came to his real agenda item. "Tell me about Agnes Nordstrom," he said. "What do you want to know?" Florence parried. Edward had noticed her habit of answering questions with a question, but then, his opening inquiry had not been very specific. It was a fishing expedition, and Florence wasn't biting.

"Every time I walk through the main catalog area downstairs, I see her at the catalog" he said. "Surely it doesn't take her all day every day to revise and check the filing of the students and clerks, does it?"

"Agnes doesn't check and revise the filing, she *does* all of the filing," Florence responded. "She *also* shifts catalog drawers as necessary, makes new labels and signs, and so on."

Edward had done his homework. "Agnes Nordstrom is a tenured associate librarian earning $38,000 a year after having been here more than twenty years. Surely that's not her job, is it?"

Florence sighed. "Agnes came here as a cataloger twenty-three years ago. Her areas were education, economics, sociology, and some of the other social sciences. She was a meticulous cataloger who took pride in her work, and she was and still is a loner. How good she was as a cataloger I can't really say. I wasn't here then, but no problems of her creation have surfaced that I know of. Automation and the development of cataloging systems changed all of the environments, as you know. When we joined OCLC and then RLN, began to work on terminals, agreed to abide by conventions and communicate with national networks of other catalogers, Agnes was a fish out of water. I don't know how hard she tried, but she was miserable and apparently she made everybody else miserable. Giving her all of the filing to do was apparently her own suggestion, and nobody had a better one. They didn't want to fire her, and perhaps they even thought that they couldn't fire her. I've talked to her a couple of times since I took this job three years ago, although of course she doesn't report to me directly. She is apparently an excellent and accurate filer, she also does odd jobs willingly, and she's as happy as can be."

Florence waited for some reaction but Edward merely took another sip of coffee so she continued. "I didn't create this present arrangement, but I continued it because I couldn't think of a better alternative. There is no way I could put her into a professional cataloging position upstairs now, it just wouldn't work out. Agnes has no intention of leaving either this library or this community voluntarily. She is planning to retire in five years. As you know we have no mandatory retirement at State U any longer, but that is what she told me. Look, Ed, it could be worse. She's at least doing something useful; the university administration has never noticed and won't as long as nobody raises the issue with them, and certainly Agnes won't. The faculty who use the catalog probably just assume she's a clerk, if they try to differentiate between librarians and clerks at all. Nobody knows, Ed."

Edward put down his coffee cup. "But we know, don't we? Furthermore, our schedule calls for freezing the present card catalog and filing no additional cards in eighteen months. What is she going to do then?"

3

THE RELUCTANT NEW SUPERVISOR

They had all agreed in the executive committee meeting that Amelia Rodriguez would be the perfect choice to be the new head of the reference department. Amelia was an excellent reference librarian, she had strong organizational and communicative skills, and she was both liked and respected by her fellow staff members and library patrons. Of course, the fact that she was Hispanic made the decision even nicer, but library director Susan Mondschein felt that they would have picked her in any case. The public library had the option of posting and advertising nationally for the job, but it didn't have to, and under the circumstances the executive committee had felt that they should just proceed with the appointment. Susan agreed.

Amelia was now in her office, and like most people Susan enjoyed being the bearer of good news. She began by telling Amelia how impressed they had all been with her performance and her attitude, and how this had led to the unanimous agreement that she should be the new head of reference. Susan went on to spell out the benefits. There would be a considerably higher salary, a nice office, a secretary, a reserved parking space. She so enjoyed telling her this that she hadn't noticed the frown starting to cloud Amelia's face.

"I'm very grateful for your kind words and the confidence being expressed in me, but I'm not sure I'm ready for a management position," Amelia finally said after waiting for Susan to finish her remarks.

Susan did not find that sort of modesty and reluctance surprising. Indeed, she was ready for it. "Of course you are! We've all been watching you for years, and you have what it takes to be a fine manager. You know the job, you know the staff and the patrons, and they all already admire and respect you. If you're worried about the mechanical requirements of the job, don't be. We're going to send you to management training programs and provide you with whatever help you need."

"I don't think you understand. It's not that I'm worried about learning the job, at least that isn't my biggest concern. I guess I could master that, with your confidence and your support. My concern is that being a manager would force me to make decisions that would affect my friends and coworkers. I would have to criticize people if they came in late, or for doing a sloppy job. I would even have to decide who got the larger raises and who got the smaller ones. I might also have to decide some day who got kept and who got laid off. I just don't think I want that sort of power over the lives of other people."

4

THE EMPLOYEE WHO WOULDN'T LEAVE

Mark Rowan was perplexed about what to do with Harry Henderson. Harry had come to the Ashboro Public Library straight from library school ten years ago. Highly recommended by his professors as an excellent student who had compiled a straight A average, Harry also had a master's degree in political science and an almost encyclopaedic knowledge of the most amazing collection of facts. He was about as close as anyone could be to what Mark, as director of the library, would call a genius. Harry had applied for and been accepted for the post of junior reference librarian; he had quickly stamped himself as the best reference librarian in the public library, to whom others passed along the toughest questions with both relief and assurance. Harry accepted these challenges with a confidence close to arrogance. He was dogged and determined, and being unable to deal with a problem simply did not enter his mind. His promotion to senior reference librarian two years later was almost routine. Typically, Harry accepted it as his due without comment.

With his superb self-driving performance also came some negative personality traits that Mark now felt he should not have so easily overlooked. If Harry wasn't arrogant he was at least somewhat supercilious. He thought, or at least his behavior suggested as much, that he was smarter and more capable than the other reference librarians, and indeed the entire library staff. He was a loner, who spent his free time attending lectures, foreign movies, and Mensa meetings, as well as reading. Although it would be fair to say he was respected and even admired, Harry was not liked.

When Adelaide Morgan had retired as head of the reference department Harry had simply come to Mark to claim the job as his due. Mark wasn't so sure. He pointed out that management required skills in dealing with people and a sensitivity Harry had not demonstrated. Harry brushed these objections aside; if there were things pertaining to management that had to be learned, he would learn them.

Mark had promoted Harry, but now realized he should not have done so. Being an excellent reference librarian and being head of reference required different skills, and while Harry possessed the former he lacked the latter. True to his word, Harry took all recommended courses and workshops, but Mark should have remembered from his own management course that while management skills can be taught, the personality factors that make for a superior manager are formed outside the classroom. Harry was certainly a "correct" head of reference, in following policies and exhibiting fairness (if being brusque to everybody could be considered fairness). He never praised his subordinates because he considered their accomplishments ordinary and obvious. He was still respected, but there was no warmth in his relationships with the reference staff, and no sense of loyalty as a two-way process. In the three years since Harry had been made head of reference, a number of what Mark had considered bright and promising (although Harry thought them all a-dime-a-dozen) junior reference librarians had left. In private discussions with Mark they had indicated that they had no sense of gratification or accomplishment from their jobs, largely because their supervisor expected everything and appreciated nothing. Mark had attempted to talk to Harry about this on a number of occasions, but it occurred to Mark that although Harry would converse he wouldn't really listen. Mark was not happy with Harry, but there was no cause—certainly under municipal civil service guidelines—that he could think of to remove him from his post.

When Harry had approached Mark about the newly vacated post of assistant director for public services, Mark was not about to repeat his mistake. He told Harry that he considered him an excellent reference librarian, but an ineffective and nonmotivating supervisor, and that he would under no circumstances consider him for this promotion, which involved not only a much higher level of management but also a considerable amount of public relations.

For the first time since Mark had known him, Harry shed his reserve and seemed genuinely angry. He told Mark that under the circumstances he saw no future for himself at Ashboro, and that he would make plans to leave as soon as possible to find a position in which he would be more appropriately appreciated. To his own surprise, Mark had felt only relief at this statement. He moved not only to fill the position of assistant director, but also began to think of restructuring moves that would affect the reference department as soon as Harry left.

But Harry had not left. The conversation had taken place nine months ago, and Harry was still here. It was possible that he had applied for other positions, but if so Mark had not heard about it as he almost certainly would have. Mark surmised that the problem, if indeed Harry was looking for another position, was a combination of his demanding and unrealistic expectations and a reputation for being difficult that had certainly begun to spread.

Moreover, besides his failure to leave, Harry had also begun to exhibit personality traits that made him even more combative and unpleasant than before. He had begun making comments in the staff lounge that were critical of the library board, his fellow administrators and the library staff, and of Mark as well, although Mark had not heard these himself. It had been reported to him by three people that Harry had characterized him as a blithering idiot, and said that as long as he was director Ashboro would never amount to any sort of library. Although he was apparently making no plans to leave, Harry talked frequently about his desire to leave, and how glad he would be to be gone.

And yet nothing seemed to happen. The newly hired assistant director for public services, to whom Harry nominally reported, looked to Mark for some action. Reorganization plans had been put on the back burner, and it seemed obvious that something had to be done. And yet, Mark countered in a debate he had with himself frequently of late, Harry was still an excellent reference librarian, and he had no other job to go to. Couldn't he be salvaged, and perhaps even salvaged for Ashboro?

5

NOT A MEMBER OF OUR TEAM

Beverly Macklin had just interviewed the second of three candidates scheduled by the city personnel office, and the third candidate would be in this afternoon. Although city personnel had nominal involvement in the hiring process of clerical staff for the public library, that office restricted itself largely to assuring that all of the legal requirements had been met, and that the applicants met the specific requirements spelled out for the job. For the position of general clerk in the pubic library those requirements were not arduous, although they included a general clerical skills test, and all applicants passed along to Beverly had to have met that requirement. Beverly, in her approach to interviewing, also looked for the intangibles: an ability to get along with fellow staff members and library patrons, a pleasant appearance and personality. These were the kinds of qualifications difficult to quantify but essential in building a staff. Fortunately for the library, Beverly knew that as far as the city personnel office was concerned she had complete freedom to select from the pool sent to her.

Beverly had felt some apprehensions about this search, because pay scales for the municipal government, and particularly for library clerical positions, did not compare to those of the business community. Yesterday's applicant had been satisfactory, but barely so, and Beverly was not enthusiastic. She would do if nobody better appeared, but that was just about all. However, this morning's candidate, Shirley Walker, had been a pleasant surprise despite Beverly's frank initial misgivings. Shirley was obviously older than the candidates she expected; indeed she had volunteered that she was 58. Probably named after Shirley Temple, Beverly thought irrelevantly. Shirley Walker was a college graduate who had not held a job after her marriage at the age of 25 and the birth of her first child. She had raised three children, had been a support to her husband in his rise through the corporate world, and had been active in club, civic, and charitable organizations. Her husband had died last year, and the children were all living in different states with families of their own. She was financially secure enough, but she needed a sense of purpose. She was healthy and enthusiastic, and had shown from her club activities that she was well organized and a good communicator. Her clerical skills were surprisingly good. She had applied specifically for this job because she had spent a good deal of time in libraries, liked them and thought they were important, and felt she could be useful here. As with the first candidate, Beverly had arranged for Shirley to talk to other staff members, and indeed would also do so for this afternoon's third candidate. However, she had to admit to herself that she liked Shirley, and unless the third candidate turned out to be quite extraordinary, Shirley Walker would be her choice.

It was at this point in her thinking that Peggy Riordan knocked on her open door and came into the room. Peggy was 25, very personable, pretty, and self-assured. All groups develop natural leaders, the people who plan the picnics, baby showers, and where to go for lunch. Peggy was clearly the leader of the library's support staff by consensus if not election. If there were a union, Peggy would almost without doubt be president or shop steward. Beverly had never had any problems with Peggy; indeed she was surprised that Peggy continued to swim in such a small pond as the public library. Peggy had the native intelligence to make a fine librarian if she had a library degree, but she had never been to college and had not expressed any interest in or expectation of promotion.

"May I speak to you for a minute, Beverly?" Peggy asked, and without waiting she continued. "The other staff members have asked me to talk to you for all of us. Are you thinking of hiring this Shirley Walker who came in for an interview this morning?"

Beverly parried the question. "Well, I haven't made up my mind. I obviously can't until the third candidate comes in this afternoon. Why do you ask?"

Peggy responded forcefully. "Shirley Walker might be nice enough if she were my aunt or maybe even my grandmother. But she wouldn't fit the staff of this library at all. She is much older than the rest of us, she is just very different in background and attitude, and we don't feel comfortable with her. You've always stressed that the library is a team. Well, we think you're right. We *are* a team, and a good team, and that's because we enjoy each other, working with each other and having fun with each other after work is over. That's why we work together so well. Shirley Walker wouldn't fit into the group at all, and we don't want her. We thought we should let you know right away, in case you were thinking about maybe hiring her."

6 CONCERN ABOUT RADIATION

After many years, the Carptown Public Library would now be automating! Carptown, a county seat in the middle of the state, was served by a library staff of twelve, including five professionals and seven full-time clerks, plus part-time students. Funding for the new automation would be coming from the state library and from federal Library Services and Construction Act money. It would allow Carptown and other small libraries like it not only to automate their circulation and cataloging systems, but to access through terminals the bibliographic holdings of other public and academic libraries in the state. The state librarian was building a network anchored on the university and large public libraries, and some level of support for document access and delivery had been promised, although some of the details were still lacking.

Library Director Minna Ferguson saw it as a great opportunity to improve library services to her patrons. Although details were sketchy, public reaction had been very positive, and the municipal government became particularly supportive once it was assured that the state was really going to pay for most of it. Initial implementation of the circulation and bibliographic access system would begin phasing in after about six months, with the arrival of the first terminals and the start of training programs.

It was at this point that Minna was visited in her office by Teri Albright. As circulation assistant (reporting to the head of the reference department), Teri would be one of the first to be trained. She was 21 and had worked in the library for the last two years. She was a good worker and well liked, and was engaged to be married in six months.

"Kenny and I have been talking about this automation for the last couple of evenings, and we decided I should speak to you right away," she said to Minna. "We've heard that exposure to radiation from computer terminals can keep a woman from becoming pregnant, and if she does become pregnant it can lead to deformed babies. We realize that none of this is scientifically certain or they wouldn't be using computers at all, but we don't want to take any chances. Kenny and I want to have children, and want to have them as soon as possible after we are married. I would like to be transferred to a job in the library where I won't have to work with computers."

7

A CIRCULATION CLERK GONE SOUR

Sandra Bellton was worried about Agnes McKenley. Actually, the whole library staff was, except perhaps for the one or two who were merely maliciously curious. But Sandra *was* worried, and not just because as director of the R & T Corporation Technical Information Center she was Aggie's boss. Agnes had worked at the R & T information center as its circulation clerk for twelve years, and indeed had worked for R & T itself for more than twenty. She had started on the assembly line, but had taken additional courses, passed a clerical aptitude test, and finally been transferred to what was then called the library in this nonunion corporation to become its circulation clerk. It was a white collar job that put her in touch with lots of people, and Aggie clearly enjoyed it. As the library had moved to automation of its circulation files and catalog access, she had adapted without a hitch.

All of that had started long before Sandra had come to R & T three years ago to head up the revitalized and growing information center, but Agnes had accepted her as she had accepted just about everything—with good nature, a wonderful sense of humor, and an infectious laugh. Aggie and her husband, Warren, who was a salesman for a local car dealership, had no children. "We raise dogs," Aggie had confided at one point. "They learn faster, they don't outgrow their clothes, and they're more grateful when you feed or pet them." Aggie and Warren didn't socialize much, at least not with anybody Sandra knew and not with others of the twelve-person information center staff. She had no really close friends at R & T, but she was friendly with just about everybody. Warren liked hunting and fishing, and either Aggie also did or she did a good job of pretending that she liked to clean fish.

The library users in particular liked her. Sandra realized that the term "circulation clerk" used by the personnel department did not really describe the importance and contribution that Agnes brought to the TIC. She was the first point of contact for the engineers, who could sometimes be a difficult and unreasonable lot, either in person or over the telephone. Even when she couldn't give them what they wanted, because the library didn't own the material or because it was charged out, or because they had to return something that somebody else needed, Aggie always got on their right side. The users sometimes called her "Sergeant" and the younger ones often called her "Mom" but it was all good-natured. Sandra recalled that once, when she herself was relatively new and Aggie was away from her desk, she had offered to help a young engineer. She had to smile now when she

8

THE DISAPPEARING PRINTER

Like many similar large public libraries, the one in Madison County had its own print shop in the basement. Although the shop was nothing spectacular in terms of modernity of equipment, and was not included in most library tours, it served the needs of the library beautifully—not only for duplicating, but also for the preparation of brochures, publicity announcements, and flyers for programs scheduled in the library auditorium. All this work could of course be done through local print shops, but usually much more slowly and always at a greater cost. When the library had started to develop this facility, there was a question as to whether there was a need, but as so often happens availability had spurred interest and volume. Many of the library departments took advantage of this opportunity, and as a result library publications not only looked professional in quality, but were on time. As a county-wide organization, the Madison Library was not required to go through the process of dealing with the municipal unions, and library director Charles Atkinson was grateful. A number of years ago the municipal union had started to make some inquiries into the possibility of organizing the library's clerical and support staff, but there had been little interest and the initiative was dropped.

Certainly Henry Hacker was not interested in unionization. An individualist best described as a character, Henry's west Texas speech patterns and accents did not even require accentuation from the cowboy boots and string tie he always wore. Henry ran the print shop as his private preserve. He kept the equipment in good running order, met the required schedules, and was always friendly even if a little flaky. Thus, when Henry announced that he would be leaving the library in three weeks, Charles was obviously concerned. Although Henry had been receiving good salary increases, Charles realized that they had really been taking the print shop for granted. Wasn't that always the way? What was that adage about the squeaking wheel?

However, Charles did not need to feel guilty. The Hackers were returning to Midland, Texas, because Henry's parents were getting on and feeling poorly. He had a chance to become a partner in a local printing business, and this was the time to take it. Charles could not really disagree. It suddenly occurred to Charles that they had no mechanism for recruiting or selecting a replacement. Henry was reassuring. They should list the job with the State Employment Office, and he himself would check around and determine the qualifications of applicants if the library wanted him to. Charles was relieved and grateful.

There were only three applicants, and of these Roger Morton both remembered how he had almost recoiled from her. "Where's Sergeant Aggie?" he wanted to know. "Isn't she here?"

All of this had begun to change slowly, starting about nine months ago. At first people did not really notice, or thought the change was temporary. Perhaps she just had a headache or an upset stomach. But the situation had continued and had gotten worse, to the point where it could no longer be ignored. Agnes, who had a string of excellent performance evaluations, was no longer excellent. In fact, in the last evaluation three months ago Sandra had stated specific criticisms, rated her as only satisfactory, and indicated that there was marked room for improvement. Agnes had declined to discuss the evaluation. She had signed and accepted it, and simply said she would try to do better. At this point, three months later, Sandra realized that the performance had deteriorated to the point where it was not satisfactory at all. A probationary employee would have been terminated, but of course both R & T and Sandra knew that Agnes deserved more consideration than that.

But how to help someone who rejected all overtures of friendship and offers of help and snapped at anyone trying to start a pleasant conversation? Sandra was of course not qualified to make diagnoses and judgments, but she could not help speculating. Agnes was now in her forties. Were the symptoms menopausal? Some of the younger staff members reported seeing Warren in local restaurants and once in a suburban motel lounge with a younger woman who did not look or act like his kid sister. However, Sandra was herself a very private person, and it was her instinctive desire to respect Aggie's clearly indicated wish for privacy. These reports were gossip, and gossip deserved to be ignored.

That was fair enough, but what about her work? Agnes McKenley's work, perhaps charitably marginal three months ago, had now deteriorated to the point where it was unsatisfactory. Her next formal appraisal was not due for another nine months. This deterioration could not be allowed to continue, for the sake of Agnes as well as the library. And as TIC director, Sandra had to look to her own responsibilities. Agnes was now curt, almost rude and surly, to the young engineers who called or came to the library. "You've got younger legs than I have. Look it up yourself!" was simply not acceptable. Her responses to questions from staff members and from Sandra herself were little better. She never initiated any conversations on her own. On her coffee breaks and lunch hours she left the building, and did not always return on time. She never shared anything at all with the group, something she had done readily, almost gregariously, until nine months ago.

Finally, in addition to her attitude, Aggie's attendance had worsened—although not to the point where disciplinary action was appropriate, at least for this by itself. An individual who had never suffered from ill health, Agnes now took a lot of sick days; indeed, she had already used up all of R & T's generous twenty-day sick-leave policy in these last nine months.

Anything after this would cut into vacation time, but she still had vacation time. She had made no plans for vacation during the summer. Usually she and Warren spent much of the summer outdoors. This year, when asked, Agnes had simply responded, "Not this summer." Her use of sick time was also odd. It did not consist of specific illnesses of several days' duration. It was simply a matter of her calling at 8 A.M. to announce that she was sick and would not be in that morning. Warren never called for her, and indeed she never received any phone calls during the days she was at work, either.

The previous week, after putting it off as long as possible, Sandra had asked Aggie to come to her office. She intended to be warm and sympathetic, but Agnes simply made that impossible. Sandra pointed to her change in attitude, her change in performance, her increased absence record. She knew she dared not pry or ask personal questions, but she did ask if there was anything wrong, said that all Agnes's co-workers were worried about her and that she wanted to help in any way she could. She pointed to R & T's fully funded physical and mental health program, including access to psychological and sociological counseling. Could Sandra make an appointment for her with any of these people? On company work time, of course.

Agnes, in her response, did not even acknowledge the concern, but fastened instead on legalism. As far as she was concerned, she was still doing her job and doing it correctly. She had been ill a lot, but she was entitled to it based on her annual sick and vacation leave, and she had not abused any privileges. She was just fine, and didn't need or appreciate any outside intervention. If Ms. Bellton (she actually reverted to calling Sandra that) had concerns about her specific job performance as spelled out in the job description, she should talk to her about that. As far as she was concerned, making jokes and smiling like an idiot was not part of the job. She then asked if there was anything else. Sandra didn't trust herself to say any more, and Agnes left the office. That was eight days ago, and there had been no change in her attitude. Today Agnes had called in sick again, and this time it would be charged to vacation time. She had been told this when she called, and her response had been typical of her recent behavior: She said she really couldn't help that, and being told wasn't going to make her suddenly better—unless somebody was suggesting she was malingering.

This couldn't go on. Agnes needed help in some way, although Sandra didn't know how to approach that issue. Sandra also knew that the situation had become untenable for the library.

looked best on paper and was the individual recommended by Henry. His employment record showed frequent job changes, but Henry pointed out that printers were often somewhat itinerant, although he didn't use that word. Morton had plausible reasons for all of his job changes, and the library's personnel department verified his present employment. That company wouldn't say much except that Morton was currently employed and doing what he claimed he was doing. However, this had become pretty standard in reference checks. Organizations provided only facts and no opinions, for fear of legal repercussions. Morton had listed his minister and another former employer as references, and Charles assumed that the personnel department had checked these out. What mattered most was that Henry Hacker confirmed that Roger Morton was an "OK guy" who knew the equipment. Charles trusted Henry; he had no expertise in interviewing and selecting printers, and obviously his experience with Henry Hacker had left him spoiled.

The library had hoped for a couple of days of overlap, but Morton insisted this would not be possible because he had to give adequate notice on his present job. That sounded fair, even responsible. Morton was scheduled to start on Monday morning, and on Friday the library had its farewell party for Henry Hacker, of whom they were all genuinely fond. He would be heading for Texas in his U-haul on Saturday.

In the middle of the festivities a call came to Charles's office from Morton's wife; Charles's secretary came to the library's lounge just as Charles was about to make his presentation, to tell him that Mrs. Morton was on the line. She wanted to know if it would be all right if her husband delayed his starting date until Wednesday. There was an urgent project with his employer that they had asked him to finish if possible. Charles knew that Henry Hacker had brought everything to a current state, had indeed bragged about the fact that he wasn't "leaving any strays to be rounded up." Atkinson told his secretary to relay the message to Mrs. Morton that Wednesday would be acceptable but no later. He didn't really think he had much choice, in any case, and he wanted the relationship to begin on a positive note.

On Wednesday morning Roger Morton failed to arrive, and telephone calls to his home went unanswered. In increasing annoyance, Atkinson called Morton's old employer on Thursday afternoon, and was told that Morton had left his old job on Friday, as scheduled. There was no knowledge or mention of any rush project to keep him longer. When Morton still had not arrived on Friday morning, Charles asked Personnel to set in motion procedures for starting a new search for someone to fill the position. The state employment service said they would check their files and call back on Monday, and the local newspaper accepted an ad for the Sunday edition. For the first time since anyone could remember, rush print jobs had to be taken on Friday to a commercial printer, where they were completed at premium prices. The Library staff, which had never complained about the print shop, started to make comments that showed their concern, and did so pointedly in the director's hearing.

Charles was at a meeting at the office of the county budget director when the call from Mrs. Morton came at 3:00 on Friday, and he found the message on his return a little after 5:00, by which time his own staff had gone. Mrs. Morton apologized for the fact that her husband had not been able to report on Wednesday as scheduled. They had been called out of town suddenly on Tuesday because her father had suffered a stroke, and lived in a city more than 600 miles away. Her father was now much improved, and they had just returned home, obviously very tired. There had been no opportunity to telephone before now, but her husband would be in to start work first thing Monday morning.

9

THE ARREST OF A MAINTENANCE EMPLOYEE

Eileen McDougall looked forward to a leisurely Sunday morning, with the local newspaper and a second cup of coffee, on her screened porch. The work week as director of the Queenstown Public Library was always hectic but usually enjoyable. Queenstown was a city of about 250,000, with the usual problems of an urban community, although it also retained a certain small-town charm. The pubic library was open on Sunday, but normally Eileen did not feel called upon to drop in. They had her number in case they really needed her. However, this Sunday she had nothing on her agenda except a 3:00 P.M. opening of the new museum exhibit, and she could even skip that if she really felt lazy. Right now, she felt very lazy and very comfortable.

The story on page 6 of the newspaper changed all that. Eileen was startled at the headline "Library Employee Arrested." She read the story several times to digest its full import, although it really said very little: Robert Hamilton, 20, an employee of the Queenstown Public Library, had been arrested on Saturday night in the downtown Washington Park on the complaint of an unidentified woman who accused him of making indecent proposals to her and trying to thrust money into her hand.

Eileen recalled that Hamilton was a member of the maintenance staff. He had worked for the library for about two years, as she remembered, and she supposed he might have come to work there straight from one of the local high schools. He was the tall, thin, polite young man who had recently moved some furniture into her office. She recalled no problems or any sort of negative information about him.

After a few minutes to collect her thoughts, she decided to call the central police station. She identified herself as the director of the library and Hamilton's employer, and asked to speak to someone familiar with the case. She was put through to Sergeant Romanelli. Romanelli was friendly and open, and it was probable that he recognized her name. He had been on desk duty when Hamilton was brought in and therefore was very familiar with the case. On weekends, he explained jovially, people at headquarters frequently pulled double shifts because the police were understaffed. The extra pay was helpful but the hours were lousy, and he would be glad to go home in about twenty minutes. She had just caught him.

Eileen was surprised that Romanelli was so communicative. After all he had only her word for who she was. Still, he obviously wasn't taking the case very seriously. Hamilton had been dumb enough, according to Sergeant Romanelli, to proposition not only the wrong woman—because there were plenty of women interested in such proposals who frequented the park—but to do so within thirty feet of a uniformed patrolman. When he was brought in, Romanelli said, Hamilton looked very scared and more than a little drunk, which might account for the whole thing. However, he hadn't been tested for alcohol or charged with being under the influence because he hadn't been driving and he wasn't abusive. Hamilton had been taken before the night court judge, who set bail at $250. His father had come down two hours later and posted bail. Hamilton was back home before dawn.

"What happens now?" Eileen asked.

"Hard to say," Romanelli said. "There probably wouldn't have been any arrest at all except for the fact that the lady was so indignant and the officer so close by. It's now up to the D.A.'s office. They might run a check on him for previous arrests. Personally I doubt they'll find anything. I have a feel for these things after all my years on the force. In any case, the D.A. might just drop the case entirely. It probably isn't worth the trouble to prosecute, unless the lady insists. Much of the time the witnesses never show up at the trial and the case has to be dismissed. If Hamilton is arraigned and pleads guilty, and if he has no previous record, the judge will probably give him a suspended sentence or probation. We don't have enough room in our city jail for hardened criminals, let alone a silly young drunk like Hamilton who can't even spot a prostitute in the park. Unless, of course, there is more to Hamilton than meets the eye. Which I doubt."

Eileen thanked Romanelli and tried to recapture the relaxation of the morning, but it was no use. The case sounded trivial enough, but that damn headline would alert the whole library staff and half the regular library users, who all worried about safety in the downtown area in which the central library was located. Why was the headline necessary? Would there have been a headline noting the arrest of a Texaco gas station attendant under similar circumstances? Eileen knew the answer, of course. The arrest of a library employee was sort of a man-bites-dog story. It was an unexpected turn of events, and the headline writer wasn't going to turn down the opportunity to get some mileage out of it in what had been an otherwise dull news evening. Nevertheless, Eileen made a mental note to gripe to Harry Davidson, the editor of the Chronicle, about it at next Wednesday's Chamber of Commerce luncheon.

As soon as she arrived the next morning Eileen asked her secretary to get Hamilton's file from the personnel department. Mavis looked at her curiously, but said nothing. Obviously she too had read the paper. By 10:30 this morning the whole library staff would know and be gossiping about it. The file added little to what she had remembered. Hamilton was single, and as she thought, he had come to the library directly from high school but continued to live with his parents. His work record was fine. Excellent attendance, excellent attitude, consistent ratings of superior. What more could you expect from a maintenance worker? However, more to the point, what would the staff, who probably hardly knew him, or the patrons, who didn't know him at all, expect? Not from Hamilton, but from her? It had been only three years since a crazed killer had murdered three young women in the downtown area before being caught, and feelings in the city were still raw.

She called Hamilton's supervisor, Tom Jacobs, and asked him to come to her office. Jacobs knew all about it, of course. He expressed himself as shocked and amazed, because Bob Hamilton was such a nice kid. He had planned to talk to Hamilton first thing this morning, but Hamilton had not come in. At this point, Eileen's secretary interrupted. "I thought you might want to see this right away. It was hand-delivered and left for you at the circulation desk." Eileen opened the envelope. The handwritten note was short and neat, even if not perfectly spelled. It said: "Dear Ms. McDougall. You have probably heard that I was arested Saturday, and I figgure you are going to fire me anyway so I'd better resign to save you the trouble. Please give my regards to my pals in maintenance and to Mr. Jacobs and let me know when I can pick up my final pay. Sincerely, Bob Hamilton."

10

TELL ME A STORY

It was only two months since her graduation from library school, but Anita Goodhue had a problem. She mused wryly that her library management course at the state university had stressed that analyzing a problem was the most difficult part, and looking for the options would be easier once the ramifications of the problem were understood. Maybe this was so virtually almost all the time, but in this case she thought she understood the problem pretty well. She just didn't know what to do about it.

Anita was a new library-school graduate, but she was not new to public libraries nor did she consider herself either immature or insensitive to management issues. What is generally called an "empty nester," Anita had worked in a variety of clerical and paraprofessional positions in her local library while the children were growing up. She understood libraries, she understood patrons, and she had often been encouraged to seek a library degree. "You really already are a wonderful librarian in everything except title," Marge Mueller, the local librarian, had often assured her. "Get a library degree! We'll support you in every way we can, certainly with release time and with tuition help if we can manage it." Anita had thought that it would be impossible, twenty years after receiving her bachelor's degree in English, and with two children and a husband at home. However, when the youngest reached high school age, she had ventured back into education a little at a time with Harry's full support and encouragement. It took her four years, but her graduation had coincided with the youngest child's heading off to college. She was ready, she was confident, and the board of the Belleville Public Library, twenty miles away and looking for a director, agreed to take her even without formal professional experience. They were willing to credit her for the intangibles she obviously brought to the job, and she wasn't going to let them down.

As she might have expected the first two months had been hectic, but there were no issues she hadn't anticipated and no problems she couldn't solve. The staff had accepted her not only as the boss but also the leader. The community was eager and responsive, the board was supportive, and her initial meetings with the mayor, the newspaper editor, the president of the chamber of commerce, and the local ministers had gone just fine. So far, so good.

Except for Marie Barnhill. Marie was the children's librarian on a professional staff of three, with the third professional the cataloger. Anita doubled in reference, and she enjoyed it. Marie had graduated from library school eight years ago, and Anita had wondered how she might feel about having a professionally junior, even if older, boss. After all, Marie had something of a reputation in children's literature. She reviewed children's books for the professional journals, and she was active in the Association for Library Service to Children. She might have been expected to show some resentment toward the newcomer. There was none. Marie had been genuinely pleasant and supportive and made it clear that she liked her own job and had no higher-level management ambitions.

And yet, something was obviously wrong. It took Anita several weeks to figure it out, but then it hit her quite suddenly. The problem was obvious, but what was the solution? Marie liked, even loved, the literature of children. She enjoyed reading and annotating the books, serving on selection juries, and writing reviews of new children's books for the Sunday paper. These were inevitably well written, and the editor had made a point, during his lunch with her, of how pleased he was with the weekly column on children's books.

Marie liked children's books. What she didn't seem to like was children! Perhaps that was unfair, but it certainly seemed that she at least felt uncomfortable with children. She spent as much time as possible in her office, with the doors closed, working on her reviews, her other writings, and her administrative duties. The children's room was not unattended, because there was a strong and loving support staff. Children, who inevitably have a much better developed instinct about people than adults do, treated Marie Barnhill with respect but not affection. They saved that for the others. Marie personally ran as few interactive programs as possible, and the result was that the kinds of innovations that occur in many public libraries Anita knew about simply didn't happen at Belleville. Perhaps others had not noticed, but certainly now that she had become aware of it, Anita could not put the issue from her mind.

Was it really possible that somebody might become a children's librarian because of a love of children's literature rather than an interest in children? Apparently. Anita thought at the first opportunity she might do a little checking at state and regional meetings to see how prevalent that phenomenon was, but the issue was obviously sensitive and she wasn't sure what to do about it even once she knew. Should she confront Marie with her concerns? If so, with what possible solution to suggest? Should she bring the issue to the board? With what recommendation—that Marie be fired? The thought was distasteful to her even as it crossed her mind. Marie was as much a victim as the children she was supposed to serve. There was no other professional post for her at Belleville. She wasn't a cataloger, and besides, that position would not be vacant. In any case, Marie considered herself a children's librarian, and a good one.

11

A CONFLICT OF VALUE SYSTEMS

Donna Martiniuk had joined the River Rapids Public Library fifteen years ago as a reference librarian. By the time Jim Graylick became director after a national search that recruited him from California three years before, Donna had already been assistant director for public services for two years.

Jim had no reason to question or second-guess the decision to promote her. Donna had been an excellent reference librarian, but beyond that she was also a natural and articulate leader to whom others looked for guidance and advice because they admired and respected her. She had been promoted to head of reference within five years of her arrival, and then to assistant director for public services. She was efficient and well organized, and she instilled both a sense of pride and a feeling of accomplishment into a group that had previously done a lot of complaining about being overworked and understaffed. They were still very busy, but Donna had persuaded them to develop a sense of purpose and to perceive these issues as opportunities rather than as problems. She gave loyalty to her staff because she fought for them when she felt they were right. She told them directly if she thought they were wrong. In return, they gave her the kind of respect and loyalty that cannot be demanded but only voluntarily granted.

Donna's husband, Al, was also well known to the library staff. He was a quiet and good-natured engineer, and they attended library functions together. They also entertained and were entertained by other members of the staff. Many of the River Rapids staff had known Donna and Al most if not all of the entire fifteen years, because there was little resident turnover in River Rapids. Everybody, including many of the library patrons, had watched the Martiniuk's only child, Emily, grow up from a precocious little girl to a charming and poised young woman.

When Emily was killed the previous year at the age of 17 in a horrible automobile accident caused by a driver judged to be totally intoxicated, all of the staff, and indeed much of the city, mourned with Donna and Al in their terrible, tragic, and senseless loss. Jim encouraged Donna to take as much time off as she needed, although he added that sometimes keeping busy helped ease or at least dull the pain. Donna had expressed her appreciation at the time, and Jim now realized how prophetic he had been. Within two weeks Donna was back at work, but it was a different Donna. The difference was not in any noticeable attitude toward the staff and patrons, to whom she continued to be polite and efficient even if not as cordial and chatty. That they could expect and understand. However, it was clear at once that Donna was a woman with a mission, and that mission was to do all she could to ensure that what had happened to her Emily would not be as likely to happen to another child and his or her parents. She threw all her energies and formidable organizing skills into the fight against drunk driving. The library staff, and Jim himself, approved enthusiastically. The cause was important, it was just, and of course it was needed therapy for Donna.

To her own surprise, Donna found that she was an eloquent, articulate, and persuasive spokesperson. She was initially featured in local newspaper stories and on TV and radio stations, and within six months she had become a national figure. She was now an officer of one of the prominent organizations engaged in this crusade; she had even become vice-chair of a group that met with the President and prominent members of Congress in the White House, a meeting that had been shown on the national evening news. One of the Sunday supplements did a feature on her, and this added to the mail and telephone messages she received. All of the library staff, and indeed all of River Rapids, were proud of what Donna had been able to accomplish for herself and this cause. Al stayed in the background. He provided the anchor in the family home and was totally supportive, but he did not participate in what had really become Donna's crusade.

All that was wonderful, but something else was inevitably starting to happen. Donna was taking more and more time away from her responsibilities as assistant director for public services at the public library. At first nobody, and certainly not Jim, had even wanted to notice, let alone say anything. Perhaps this was a surge of activity that would run its course. Jim was really not sure how much others had seen and pretended not to see, but he was director of the library and it was his responsibility. Her absences continued to increase. Donna simply took the time off whenever it was needed, leaving a message with her secretary to pass along to the director. Jim calculated that during the last two months Donna had been away from the library at least 50 percent of the time. Discreet inquiries into the workings of the public services department, not difficult because he could justifiably discuss issues with her subordinates during her absences, disclosed that much of her work simply wasn't getting done at all, much as others tried to cover up for her. Certainly nobody complained to Jim, but he realized that management reports were not only late but hadn't even been started, and that planning and staff development activities, in which Donna had always excelled and taken pride, had simply been shunted aside.

Jim felt that it was his management responsibility to talk to Donna. He was aware of the sensitivity of the situation. He planned to proceed slowly and carefully, trying to make Donna see for herself that she had to make some priority decisions. There were, of course, options, ranging all the way from an agreement on the level of her outside activity, to a relinquishing of her administrative responsibilities for a time, to switching to a part-time position, to a leave of absence. All of these were acceptable to Jim, and he had planned to put some of them on the table. Indeed, he was ready to listen to any suggestions that Donna might have to offer. He counted on their friendship and her balanced and intelligent approach to issues, as well as on her loyalty to the library, to create a productive meeting.

He had been terribly wrong. The meeting was a disaster from the start. Donna simply cut him off before he had barely begun, stating that she found it monstrous that he was talking about something as trivial and fleeting as library schedules when she was trying to save lives, to save other children and other parents from what the Martiniuks had been forced to endure. In any case she insisted that she was getting all of her work done by taking things home with her in the evenings. She added that she worked past midnight in hotel rooms and on airplanes. Jim knew that this wasn't totally successful even if true, but that in any case the paperwork wasn't the only issue. The assistant director for public services had to be at the library in person much of the time; she had to participate in staff planning meetings, to interact with subordinates and with patrons in formal and spur-of-the-moment sessions, and to do the thousand and one things that could never be included in any administrator's job description because they involved problem recognition and problem attention as issues arose.

However, he never got a chance to say any of this because Donna, with the experience and confidence of many public speaking appearances, just went on talking in cold and measured tones: As she had already noted, she saw no problem in combining her outside activities dealing with the scourge of drunken driving with her responsibilities as assistant director for public services. She had assumed that the library director would be supportive. Still, if he was concerned that she was taking advantage of the library she would simply, after taking all of her accrued vacation, take leave without pay for the additional absences. That should satisfy him. Whatever happened, she would not turn down any opportunities to do some real good. Having said this, she gave him a cold glance and without another word left the room.

Jim sat there for a long time in embarrassed frustration that slowly turned to anger. The issue obviously wasn't saving the money, and Donna was certainly smart enough to have understood this. He had been manipulated and made to look like an insensitive piker, when all he really wanted was what the library needed, an assistant director who would do the job. He wondered if he hadn't made a mistake in talking to Donna without first discussing the issue with the board of trustees, or even the mayor. The board, he realized, felt only sympathy for Donna and pride for her courage. They were not aware of any library operational problems.

12

I BEFORE E EXCEPT AFTER C

Library director Charles Hastings of Gigantic State University contrived to take another accidental walk past Donna Washington's desk, but he found exactly what he had found for the last two weeks. Donna was discreetly reading a magazine. Hastings couldn't understand it. Donna had been hired four months ago in response to repeated agitation from his staff about getting them more secretarial support. The complaints, he knew, had validity. He had surrounded himself with a bright group of people who took the responsibilities of professional involvement seriously. That meant correspondence, speeches, and articles. Hastings had his own secretary, of course, and there were other support people who served the assistant directors and helped them to generate university memoranda and reports. However, the staff people at a slightly lower level were hurting for support when it came to anything beyond the regularly assigned job duties.

Adding an additional position to the already stretched library budget, particularly in a support capacity, would have been difficult. However, Hastings was proud of the innovative way in which he had solved the problem. The university had a commitment. The personnel department had been working closely with an inner-city training program that prepared young high school graduates (and sometimes not-so-young dropouts and returnees) for the office job market. The training provided varied with the skills being taught, but when Hastings had asked for a qualified typist (he thought that demanding computer skills might be pushing things) who could also use dictaphone equipment, the personnel department indicated this might be possible. He had broached the idea at his own staff meeting, and the response had been unanimously and enthusiastically positive. They saw no difficulty in using dictaphones for their correspondence, and in using that approach and rough copy for generating drafts and eventually final copy for speeches and papers. Moreover, they were as pleased as he at the ability to do something besides providing lip service to the concept of minority hiring. The sea of white faces in the library administrative wing disturbed them as much as it did him. Having the university provide the funds made things just about perfect.

On that basis Donna Washington had arrived four months ago. A single mother in her early twenties, she had made an acceptable score on the typing test, and she knew how to handle a dictaphone. In addition she was bright, alert, cooperative, and cheerful. Everybody liked her at once. And indeed, for the first few weeks she had waded with enthusiasm into the accumulated backlog of work. He had seen for himself that she was a willing worker and a hard worker. And now she was just sitting there reading magazines! Something was wrong.

Hastings made one more "accidental" detour past Donna's desk, but this time he decided to stop and say something. "Not too busy today, Donna?" he inquired casually. He did not mention that she had apparently not been busy for weeks.

Donna looked a little flustered. "Things have been kind of quiet recently, Mr. Hastings. I keep checking around, but nobody has anything for me right now. They say things will pick up pretty soon. I've stayed at my desk to help answer the phone, but I thought it would be all right to bring in a magazine. The days go slowly when there isn't enough to do. I'd much rather be busy. I'm sure everybody would." Hastings added his agreement that things would certainly pick up pretty soon and returned to his office. However, he decided to bring up the issue at his staff meeting on Friday to the twelve professionals in the administrative office.

Hastings was blunt and direct. He wanted to know why, after complaining incessantly about the need for clerical support, they now had no work for Donna. There was an embarrassed silence, and Hastings was aware of the fact that everybody was avoiding his eyes. Finally Marilyn Romagno, the library systems officer, spoke up. "She can't spell, Charley. We've tried correcting her work and giving it back to her, but it always comes back with other mistakes. I've just decided it's easier to do it all myself." There was a murmur of agreement around the room, but nobody else spoke.

"Look," Hastings said. "Everybody has trouble with spelling sometimes. I know I do. That's why we have dictionaries." He attempted a small laugh, but there was no rejoinder.

"You don't understand," Marilyn said. "She can't spell at all. I know we use specialized nomenclature and acronyms, and I would understand if those gave her trouble at first. But Donna can't spell the simple everyday words either. Apparently she never learned how in school in the first place."

Hastings considered this bit of news. It was true that an ability to copy rapidly from prepared text, which is what typing tests are, differs from dictaphone transcription because it does not require spelling skills. Nobody expects the candidate to check the spelling on a test form. In that sense what Marilyn had said seemed plausible. He simply had not anticipated this, and he wondered whether the university's personnel department had. The staff at the inner-city training program should have, he felt.

He was becoming angry. "How long has this been going on?" he demanded.

Ron Buchwald, the library's fund-raising and development officer, apparently felt that Marilyn had taken enough heat. Even in his state of annoyance Hastings noted with pleasure that his staff were a close-knit bunch who worked well together and supported one another.

"We've all known from almost the first day, Charley," Ron admitted. "At first we thought that if we pointed out her mistakes things would get better. But they really didn't. She sometimes remembers the same word the next time, but there are an awful lot of words out there." Ron had tried a little levity, but nobody joined in and he quickly resumed a serious tone. "I guess we've all just decided that giving her this work is more trouble than it's worth. It's not that she doesn't care or try. She does. Donna is a sweet kid, and she wants very much to please us. She's probably figured out that something is wrong, but I'm not sure she knows what it is."

This was really the last straw for Hastings. He had uncovered a conspiracy of silence that, as best he could tell, involved everybody but himself. He felt somehow betrayed, and he said in the icy voice he used when he was really upset, "You've known this all along, but nobody said anything to me about it. I want to know why!"

"It's really very simple," Ron replied. "We knew that if we told you that she couldn't do the work you would have no choice but to fire her. We wanted to protect her at least until the end of her six months probationary period, and then tell you that the university would have to find her something else to do, because she couldn't work here."

13 WITHHOLDING OF INTERLIBRARY LOANS

"I need to show you something," public services assistant director Anita Bergland said to library director Marcus Henson, and Henson dutifully followed Bergland down to the interlibrary loans office. "We came across this strictly by accident," Bergland explained. "Susan Reardon, who as you know heads interlibrary loans, has been sick the last two days, and we were looking for some correspondence we couldn't find. We opened the bottom drawer of her desk and found these." What Bergland withdrew from the drawer was a stack of perhaps twenty or more interlibrary loan request forms, dating back as much as nine months. It was obvious that these had not been filled out and were just put into the drawer. All of the requests were from libraries in the Republic of South Africa, except for one that was from a right-wing country in Central America. The common denominator appeared to be the perception that both countries violated human rights.

Since this was a state university and policy made by the board of trustees, Henson was troubled by this discovery. There had been agitation on the campus for complete divestment of stock holdings with companies that traded in South Africa, but the board had chosen to maintain what it called a modified stock portfolio of companies that, in the board's judgment, made a positive contribution to the needs of blacks in South Africa by their presence. This did not satisfy the protesters, and recent board meetings had been picketed. In addition, the university had a program of educational cooperation with a black pre-college institution in South Africa, whose intent it was to prepare black students for entry into institutions of higher education that had begun to accept black students, such as Cape Town and Witwatersrand. Two of the requests had come from this small institution, the others from more traditional South African universities. Henson was concerned because any attempt to withhold information in this manner appeared to him contrary to both university and library policy, since neither body had ever promulgated regulations to exclude any request on the basis of nationality. The library quite routinely filled requests from Eastern Europe and from the People's Republic of China.

When confronted by this accidental discovery on her return to work two days later, Susan Reardon was anything but contrite. "I'm glad you found them, and I'm just sorry I didn't have the guts to tell you in advance what I was doing. My job as a librarian does not override my responsibilities as a human being. I am not going to provide assistance to any kind of government that kills and terrorizes its own people, and I never will. Furthermore, the ALA has passed resolutions urging us to enforce the boycott on sending informational materials to South Africa. Don't you even support your own profession?"

Marcus was taken aback by the vehemence of Susan's position. He had expected a plea for agreement, perhaps even an apology. Susan was a fine librarian, and in her eight years at the library he had not even been aware of any political involvement on her part. Marcus knew he did not want to have this develop into a public debate. The student newspaper would pounce on the story, given half a chance; the publicity could polarize the library staff, and the university administration would not appreciate his giving the protesters one more tool.

14

FREE SEARCHING FOR THE POOR

Sybil Thornbush was quite sure that the income from data-base searching did not match the invoices she was seeing from the data-base vendors. Library policy was to absorb labor and hardware costs, but to pass along to the public library's clients the cost of actual connect time. The two figures didn't match; they weren't even close. Since Jeff Martinovich did virtually all of the on-line searching, the simplest thing to do would be to ask him. Jeff had been at the public library for nine months, and he had come straight out of library school. He was bright, articulate, committed to his profession, and an excellent reference librarian. Sybil felt she had made a good choice in selecting Jeff.

In his response to her question, Jeff was direct. "I'm glad you found out. I'm only ashamed I didn't tell you on my own, and I apologize for that. But I don't apologize for what I am doing. I don't really believe we should be charging for on-line searching at all. Reference work is reference work, no matter how it's done. However, I know it's library policy to charge, and so I have been doing that. However, when somebody can't afford to pay I waive the fee."

"And how do you know they can't afford to pay the fee?" Sybil almost felt she sounded like Walter Cunningham, board chairman and local bank president.

"I really don't know," Jeff responded. "I take their word for it. People wouldn't lie about a thing like that. Besides, a lot of them are students in the local college, and I can remember what it was like working my way through library school while living on macaroni and cheese. I couldn't have paid for on-line searches then, and I'm sure most of the students can't afford it now. Besides, you know that it's wrong to charge for public library services in any case. The American Library Association has said so over and over, and so has the state library association. I'm already compromising my principles as it is."

Sybil felt a wave of recognition and sympathy for Jeff's arguments. So young and so idealistic, as she once was! She tried to be patient. "All of this was fought out with the library board a number of years ago, before you came here. The board subsidizes all but the direct out-of-pocket costs, but there are to be no exceptions. That is the best I could get, and those are the rules."

"Well, then, perhaps we shouldn't be doing on-line searching at all," Jeff almost shouted. "Library services are free, and if we can't offer them for free, we shouldn't offer them."

"And whom does that help?" Sybil responded quietly. "The people with enough money can still get all the on-line searches they want from commercial organizations, and the library becomes less relevant for the whole community. We need to do on-line searching, and I took it on the terms I could get it. Maybe you think I was wrong, but it was my decision to make, and I think I made the right one. I promise you that we'll fight this out again with the board another day. Maybe after Walter Cunningham retires and moves to Arizona at the end of next year."

Jeff had also become quiet. "I'm sorry I lost my composure, Sybil, and I understand what you're saying. I don't blame you at all. However, I don't think I can be a professional librarian and turn people away from needed services because they don't have any money. If that's going to have to be the rule here then perhaps I can't stay here as a reference librarian."

15

THE USE OF A PARKING SPACE

Bernie Holovak, the director of the Kentville Public Library, knew that his secretary, Shirley Clifton, was not well liked by the other secretaries on the library staff. Part of this came perhaps from the fact that Shirley was older and shared few of their interests. However, part of it could be ascribed to a personality that some would call efficient and others might describe as officious. Shirley never let the other support staff people forget that she worked for the director, and that this gave her a special status in the library. She might be a nonlibrarian, but she nevertheless claimed for herself a unique status that simply radiated through her personality.

Bernie was aware of all this, but he didn't worry about it very much. Shirley was rather cold and humorless, even to him, but she was efficient at what she did. She was superb at handling the secretarial skills of shorthand, typing, and filing, but beyond that she functioned increasingly as an administrative assistant in scheduling meetings, handling routine matters and referring those who did not require his direct intervention, and knowing what calls to put through directly and what calls to defer for a later return. She had an unfailing instinct for what and who was important. She had now worked for Bernie for twelve years, and while there was no personal warmth in their relationship, they were an efficient team. They remembered each other's birthdays, and he brought her a plant for National Secretaries Week and her favorite perfume for Christmas. That was about it. Shirley was in her fifties and single; she enjoyed gardening, crocheting, and classical music, but since none of these interested Bernie they never talked about them. Bernie's wife had attempted to become friendly with Shirley when she called on the phone or visited the office, but after a while she had just given up. Shirley was not rude, she was just cold and disinterested, and if she acted toward some people as though she felt superior maybe it was because she did feel that way.

In any case, she was an excellent secretary. As Bernie had become involved in professional and civic associations, and now served as a board member for the Boy Scouts of America, she had taken on increasing responsibilities, particularly in view of his growing number of out-of-town trips. The library board had encouraged his outside involvements as long as there were no adverse impacts on the library but he had excellent assistant directors and he certainly had a competent secretary. All of this gave Bernie a great deal of freedom.

When the reference department secretary intercepted him in the hallway one morning and asked if she and several of the other secretaries could speak to him for a few minutes, it did not occur to him that they had specifically picked a day when Shirley was on vacation. That realization came later. He asked Judi what they wanted to talk to him about, and she had just said "parking."

Parking was a big problem for the Kentville Public Library staff, and he didn't really have any solutions in mind. However, he realized that if staff members felt they had a problem he had to be willing to talk about it. This morning was not too busy, and so he had told Judi he could give them about fifteen minutes at 10:30. Judi had said that fifteen minutes would be enough. As he waited for them, Bernie reviewed the policies in his mind. They were quite simple. There were four parking spaces next to the library building, and these were assigned to the director and the three assistant directors. There was a parking lot for library users, but staff members were not supposed to use this because if they did they would simply fill up all the spaces. The staff understood and complied. All the other employees had to park in the municipal lot. Parking there was by permit and free for city employees, but the lot was two blocks from the library and unpaved. When it rained, or in the winter with a lot of snow on the ground, there was a good deal of griping. However, that griping wasn't restricted to library employees. In any case, if the professional librarians except for the assistant directors also had to park out there, surely the secretaries couldn't have a complaint, Bernie thought.

When the four secretaries (Bernie recognized that they were all at the department level and that they were all in their twenties) filed into his office, Bernie tried to make them comfortable, because it was obvious they were ill at ease. He reviewed the policy on parking for them, told them of the hopes for paving the municipal parking lot (which he knew was probably more a dream than a hope), and finally asked what had brought them.

"It's Shirley," Judi said quite directly. "She's a secretary just like us, and she's supposed to park in the municipal lot like the rest of us. That's fair. Even my boss parks out there and she's the head of the reference department. Shirley thinks she's more important than the rest of us. When you're out of town she just parks in your parking space. We don't know whether or not you told her that was okay, but in any case we don't think it's fair. If you want to make your space available when you're out of town, you should rotate it. Otherwise leave it empty."

Bernie had not known Shirley was using his parking space when he was on trips. However, he realized immediately how easy it was for her to do so. She, uniquely among all the library staff members because she made his travel arrangements, knew when he would be there, when he would be out of town, and when he would return.

16

A CONFLICT OF INTEREST?

Tom Donovan, director of the library at Quantum University, was pleased with the changes he had made since coming to Quantum five years ago. While the Quantum library was still a strong collection of research materials, it was his impression that there was something of a smug sense of comfort about the place. With the full support of the president, Tom had made changes in personnel as opportunities presented themselves. These employees had not only started some dynamic new initiatives, they had also challenged and examined historic procedures.

Jill Monroe was the kind of individual Tom had in mind. Bright, alert, young, and assertive, Jill combined an understanding of traditional approaches and values with a keen sense both of management techniques and of the evaluation and application of technology. One of her first actions two years ago had been to question the arrangement under which the library's periodical subscription business was routinely awarded to the Safeco Subscription Agency. Safeco was the largest in the country, and there had been no complaints about its service. However, Jill noted that some of the other subscription agencies offered technological interfaces that could speed the communication process and save Quantum internal labor costs. Moreover, a competitive bidding to match new and tightened specifications might even reduce the service fees that Quantum had traditionally paid. Safeco had assured them that the service charges were fair and consistent, and that was that. Jill, in contrast, didn't much care whether they were fair or consistent. She wanted them low, and she wanted additional service parameters.

And so it was that after over ten years of uninterrupted Safeco service, the review committee appointed by Jill had recommended to her that Quantum move its subscription business to the Communico agency. Communico was a younger and smaller company, but its proposal had been excellent, and the cost reductions were real enough. In the year since all of this had happened, there had been complete satisfaction with Communico's performance, and the decision that had at one point seemed rather risky was vindicated.

Tom Donovan reviewed all of this in his mind as he reread the letter he held in his hand. It was a typed letter, and it was anonymous. Tom had an instinctive distaste for correspondence from individuals unwilling to sign their names. Nevertheless, what the letter contained could not simply be dismissed and ignored. It said: "Dear Dr. Donovan: Are you aware of the fact that Jill Monroe, who engineered the switch from Safeco to Communico, is a very, very good friend (if you know what I mean) of the president of the Communico Corporation, and was even before she came to Quantum? In fact, last spring on her skiing holiday she stayed as a personal houseguest in his vacation home in Aspen, Colorado." The envelope had of course no return address. It was postmarked in the city. Tom surmised that it might be a library staff member, perhaps a staff member with a grudge against Jill Monroe.

Donovan did not make it a practice to delve into the personal lives of his staff members. He felt that this was none of his business, and that his task was to evaluate performance. He did know that Jill Monroe was vivacious, single, and in her late thirties. She enjoyed skiing, and had indeed taken a one-week vacation for that purpose in Colorado last March.

17 JUST WORK; DON'T ASK SO MANY QUESTIONS!

Library school dean Emory Woolcott was happy to receive the call from Sheila Meyer. In a long career in library education, Emory couldn't remember all of his students very well, but he tended to remember the excellent ones; the ones who had shown the promise of becoming superb librarians and professional leaders. Sheila was such an alumna. Although she had graduated only nine months ago, Emory was positive that the combination of her academic knowledge, her intelligence, and her outgoing personality would lead to good things. Sheila had been a student in his management class, and he remembered her warmly. He had stressed to her, as indeed he stated to all graduates at the farewell luncheon, that he hoped they would stay in touch and that he would be happy to talk to them at any time. As he waited for his secretary to transfer the call, Emory Woolcott looked forward to a pleasant chat. Sheila had come to library school with a masters degree in history, and had performed with distinction in the pursuit of her M.L.S. She was already a member of Phi Beta Kappa when she came, and had now also qualified for Beta Phi Mu, the library science honorary society.

Sheila had many career specialization options; indeed Emory hoped at some point to see her in a management post, because she had both a quick grasp of issues and a pragmatic approach to their solution. However, Sheila had wanted to be an academic library cataloger from the start. Because there was and is a shortage of qualified catalogers for research libraries, Sheila had many interview opportunities, and she had discussed some of these with him. She had ultimately chosen to accept a junior cataloging post at Wentworth University. Emory knew little about Wentworth, which was 2,000 miles away. He knew it was a major private university of distinguished academic ranking. Its library was not a member of the Association of Research Libraries, but he guessed that they weren't far from qualifying. The director of the library, Henrietta Turnbull, was somebody he did know. Henrietta was active and visible in the profession. She had served on the executive board of the American Library Association, and as president of the Association of College and Research Libraries. She was a frequent speaker and writer, particularly on issues of management, and was considered a bright light in the profession. Emory did not know anyone in technical services at Wentworth. That was not his area.

When he received the telephone call from Sheila, it became immediately clear that this was not going to be a pleasant chat. She was deeply troubled, and her concern centered on her relationship with the head of monographic cataloging, Adelaide Fontanna, her direct supervisor. "Adelaide has never been angry or abusive to me," Sheila explained. "That's not her personality at all. In fact she has been very pleasant and courteous from the start. It's just that her attitudes are so old and set, even though she's only about 45. She kind of treats me like a daughter, and I know she's trying to be kind and helpful, but I already have a mother and I'm really looking more for a colleague and teacher." Emory had a pretty good idea of the type that Sheila was describing but decided not to interject, because Sheila was under full sail, her frustrations tumbling out.

"When I started here six months ago, Adelaide explained all the policies and procedures to me very carefully. She urged me to come to her with any questions I might have, but I soon understood that she meant questions of how and not of why. Well, I had both! You and the cataloging faculty have always stressed to me that procedures and policies should be questioned and reviewed. Obviously, Adelaide never took any courses from any of you.

"Wentworth has cataloging policies that appeared to me to be slow, cumbersome, and in some cases unnecessary. It also has a big cataloging backlog, and it seemed to me that might be why. I wasn't trying to cause trouble, Dr. Woolcott, I was just trying to bring a new perspective. You've always taught us that sometimes people can be too close to a problem to see possible alternatives."

Emory stepped in to reassure Sheila that she had done nothing wrong or abnormal, and she continued. "I realized almost from the first that Adelaide did not appreciate my raising questions she considered a challenge to her management decisions, but I really tried never to suggest that. Anyway, raising questions where appropriate is the job of any professional.

"Adelaide always answered my questions slowly, carefully, and calmly. Sometimes her answers made sense and clarified the reasons, and I always made it a point to thank her for explaining the issue to me. However, many of the policies and cumbersome procedures didn't seem to have any reasons, at least none she would or could explain. On those occasions she just simply told me that this was the way things had always been done and *would* be done under her direction in monographic cataloging. I guess she could see from my face that I didn't consider this much of an answer. I don't dislike her, Dr. Woolcott, I just don't respect her very much. To be honest, I don't really respect her professional attitude at all. To me, she represents all of the stereotypes that people warned me about. Before Adelaide I had never met any catalogers like that. Maybe I was just lucky. In any case, one of the reasons I became a cataloger is to change that perception of what catalogers are and do.

"The reason I'm calling you, Dr. Woolcott, is because of what happened this morning. Adelaide asked me to come to her office, shut the door, and sit down. She told me she liked me, and that she thought I had a lot of promise as a cataloger. She also told me that there was still a lot I didn't know, and that I should give some credit to her twenty years of experience. She made the policies and procedures for monographic cataloging, and our job was to reduce the backlog and at the same time do a high quality job. She was not an unreasonable or arbitrary person, she said, but she also felt that after just a few months my comments were not based on very much knowledge, and only tended to be disruptive. She suggested strongly that I should perhaps consider doing things her way for a year or two, before I considered myself qualified to question policies.

"Dr. Woolcott, I know I've only worked there about half a year, and that nobody should change professional positions so quickly. And I really like everything else about Wentworth and the rest of the staff. But I can't work under such rules, where I am expected not to think and evaluate but just to grind out the work under procedures that I think are cumbersome and sometimes just plain stupid. I really hope you can advise me what to do."

18

FEAR OF FLYING

Ingeborg Dahlstrom, dean of libraries at Golden State University, was very pleased at the letter she had just received. From the Library of Congress, it invited Golden State to appoint a representative to a new blue ribbon LC Committee that would advise in the planning and implementation of the Library of Congress's own implementation of advanced computer systems, and particularly in their integration into national networks of data-base and resource sharing. It would be a committee of twelve, carefully selected.

Ingeborg knew why Golden State, certainly not one of the dozen largest academic libraries in the country, had been selected for this great honor. It was because of the advanced and immensely successful work in library systems development and implementation, particularly as it affected technical services and resource sharing, that had been pioneered at this beautiful campus nestled on the western slopes of the Sierra Nevada. She also knew who was responsible for this accomplishment, and the attendant honor just bestowed. It was Frank Hernandez, associate dean for library systems and technology. Frank had come to the university five years before, and what he had accomplished had been truly amazing, both in terms of technical development and in the ability to persuade others in the university and the library to participate in and support this endeavor. Clearly, Frank was the individual to represent Golden State on this advisory committee. It was a great honor for Golden State, and it was both a great and a deserved honor for Frank Hernandez.

She had called Frank to her office to give him the good news. She reported what was in the letter, which also included the information that the committee would meet four times a year in Washington. She added how pleased she was, how it was obvious that they had received this invitation because of him and that therefore he was the clear choice for the appointment, and that of course Golden State would support all travel and lodging expenses for this meeting that might not be covered by the Library of Congress.

However, instead of sharing her elation and exuberance, Frank looked troubled. He allowed her to finish, and then he spoke slowly. "I really appreciate this honor for Golden State, and your confidence in asking me, but I can't accept. I am not able to commit to these trips to Washington because I don't fly."

Ingeborg tried to laugh it off. "I know what you mean. With delays, crowded airplanes, tasteless food, and misplaced luggage, I don't know anyone who enjoys flying. I certainly don't."

Frank did not return her smile. "You don't understand. I don't fly because I *won't* fly. I'd better explain. I used to fly, both for business and pleasure, until twelve years ago. That's when my father was killed when the plane crashed on landing while my mother and I were waiting at the airport. Since that time, I can't even drive past an airport without getting sick to my stomach. I won't, I can't fly, and I know that this is the only way to get to Washington for meetings. You'll have to appoint somebody else, or LC will have to find a substitute university."

All of this was news to Ingeborg. She suddenly recalled that Frank had never attended any ALA meetings that weren't on the West Coast, and that while he had written papers he rarely presented them in person. She had assumed that this was because of some combination of being very busy and perhaps being shy. It all suddenly made sense.

She did not really think that anyone else could represent Golden State on this committee. Turning down the invitation would appear strange, but perhaps it could be explained and it was in any case not crucial. Not for the library or for her. However, an unwillingness to travel by air would most certainly put a severe crimp into the professional career development of Frank Hernandez, one of the brightest people in a rapidly developing area of the profession.

She was no expert, but she knew that his abhorrence of flying was caused by a severe emotional reaction to his father's death, and she was confident that psychological counseling could help him overcome this blockage as it had helped many other reluctant flyers. She wasn't thinking of the library now, she was thinking of Frank Hernandez.

19

BYPASSED FOR PROMOTION

The library's associate dean for administration and personnel, Marianne Hoogedoorn, had a pretty good idea about why cataloger Deborah Higdon had sought an appointment, but it was better not to guess, and it was important to let Deborah state her complaints. In the absence of a union, personnel departments play the role of union shop stewards as well as policy interpreters; therefore, protecting employees when they have a legitimate grievance is as important as explaining to them why their complaint is not considered reasonable.

"You probably know why I'm here," Deborah began rather nervously. "I've been at this university for over twenty years. My performance evaluations as a cataloger have always been at least satisfactory, and at times superior. At that, I have always felt I was being shortchanged. I've worked very hard, putting in extra hours that often were neither acknowledged nor even noticed. I haven't minded doing that. We have a large backlog, and I want to do my share. I have done that, in fact I've done *more* than my share.

"But that isn't why I'm here. As you know, the position of assistant head of monographic cataloging became vacant through resignation three months ago. When Frances Schimmel, the head of cataloging, announced that it would be filled through internal promotion, I just naturally assumed that I would receive this promotion. I have the most seniority, and I think

I can state confidently that I know more about the cataloging procedures in this university than anyone else. When it was announced that the promotion would go to Lucy Pocock, I was shocked beyond words. Lucy has only been here for four years! She is bright and I like her, but I've forgotten more about cataloging than she will probably ever know. This is a terrible snub and a terrible insult. I just don't see how I can accept it, remain here, and keep my self-respect."

Deborah realized that she might be losing control, so she stopped. She swallowed, blinked, and looked at Marianne for some reaction. Marianne decided to proceed gently. "Surely you've discussed your feelings and concerns with Frances, haven't you?" Deborah nodded. "What did she tell you by way of explanation?" asked Marianne.

"She told me that there was more to being a supervisor than being a dependable cataloger. She said that Lucy had been involved professionally, had presented papers at ALA and at regional conferences, and had even taken a number of continuing education courses dealing with both technical services and personnel administration. She told me that the position of assistant head of cataloging involved more than cataloging skills. It required a level of recognition and participation outside the confines of just this library. She told me that Lucy had all of these attributes, and I didn't."

"Do you think these requirements that Frances enumerated are reasonable?" Marianne pressed gently.

"Perhaps yes, perhaps not all of them. That's not the point. Frances has been my boss for over ten years. We have probably had thousands of conversations in that time, and hundreds of cups of coffee in the library cafeteria. I've been to her house, and she's been to mine. I considered her a friend as well as a colleague. Never in all that time did she ever suggest to me that I should be doing any of the things she is now accusing me of not doing. Never in ten years was I ever told that my priorities were wrong. Frances simply let me go on working my head off, spending extra hours on the backlog. Maybe I was wrong in not asking her what it took to become assistant head, but wasn't she also wrong in never even asking me what my objectives were? I know now that I have been foolish in assuming an appreciation I never received, but feeling foolish also makes me feel angry. I think I've been betrayed. Not just by Frances, although it starts with her, but by all of you, by this whole library administration."

20
AN ALLOCATION OF MERIT INCREASES

In one sense the problem was simple. At least it was mathematically simple. Fred Plunkett, manager of the Biotronics Technical Information Center, had just received word from the director of research, who was his immediate boss, that an average of 8 percent would be available for salary increases for professional staff, or, in other words, employees exempt under the provisions of the Fair Labor Standards Act. The other employees, who used to be but no longer were called clerks but who were in any case nonexempt, would receive standard across-the-board salary increases. Biotronics did not have a clerical union that would have demanded such increases, but it acted as though it did. Perhaps this was perceived as the best way to head off unionization.

In dealing with professionals, however, Biotronics not only expected differentiations based on performance, it expected its managers to use salary increases as a tactic for reward and encouragement on the one hand and for sending a message of greater expectations on the other. The director of research had stated that cost of living should be factored into the increase pattern, but that he definitely expected to see some application of merit approaches. An "average" of 8 percent applied to dollars. Fred was expected to give deserving subordinates a greater than 8 percent raise, but to do that he had to give others a smaller increase.

The issue was simple in the sense that Fred had only three professionals to evaluate. The complication would come into play because in such a small group, the cause and effect of salary decisions would be immediately apparent. Fred considered his options. He was not only pleased but really in one sense surprised by the performance of Anna Bancroft, the cataloger (or, as she was called, technical information analysis specialist). Anna had come to Biotronics sixteen years ago, and a relatively modest increase might therefore seem in order for an individual in the same position for such a considerable length of time. However, Anna had made some remarkable adjustments. During the last two years, she had handled the switch into the OCLC network without a hitch; and her ability and willingness to share resources with others had not only increased her productivity, but it had led her to volunteer that a clerk who had just resigned to relocate to another part of the country need not be replaced. Fred was impressed, because that sort of thing rarely happened.

Fred was also pleased with the performance of Terri Bergolini, the literature searcher. Terri had a master's in physics and her M.L.S., and she had come to Biotronics two years ago straight out of library school. She handled both retrospective searches and selective dissemination of information (SDI) for a wide range of users, and Fred had received nothing but positive reactions to her work. Fred knew she was good, as well as highly regarded. As a young single woman with a strong combination of degrees, Fred knew that she was also professionally mobile. Her involvements in the Special Libraries Association would certainly bring her outside job opportunities. Perhaps they already had.

Fred was less pleased with Marybeth Chadwick. Marybeth had come to Biotronics eight years ago, although she had worked as a librarian for more than twenty. She handled the more traditional reference functions, both in person and over the telephone. Her work was adequate, but that was about all. Library patrons had expressed no particular support for her rather dour personality. She had taken no initiatives and suggested no changes, and she had not participated in outside professional activities. In contrast to the others, she was a chronic complainer and griper, who felt overworked and pressured, given her regular workload and the fact that she had to supervise both the circulation clerk and the interlibrary loan clerk. Two months ago, sensing that the interlibrary loan clerk was receiving very little direction and supervision from Marybeth, Fred had assigned her to report to Terri. In one sense this made sense in any case. While some interlibrary loans resulted from direct requests to Marybeth, others resulted from Terri's literature searches. Marybeth accepted the change with some relief and an "it's about time somebody else did something" kind of attitude. Terri accepted the new responsibility without objections. As far as Fred could determine, theses changes had worked out quite well.

As Fred contemplated his options, he decided on a 9 percent increase for Anna, a 10 percent increase for Terri, and a 5.5 percent increase for Marybeth. It came out a to a little more than an average of 8 percent for the pool (his own salary increase would be determined separately by the director of research), but he felt he could justify the difference to his boss. An increase of 5.5 percent would send the message to Marybeth that he was not completely pleased, but would also keep her salary in step with inflationary cost increases.

He was about to put his recommendations into writing, when Marybeth Chadwick entered Fred's office. She had just heard of the professional salary increase allocations for the corporation from a friend in the personnel department (Marybeth had always had an excellent grapevine), and she wanted to know what sort of increase he planned to recommend for her. Without waiting for an answer, Marybeth went on to state that she expected an increase of at least something above the average. She had had to work much harder than the others and under much greater pressure, because she was the only one of the three unable to plan what she was going to do when. For this reason any comparison involving professional participation and innovation would be unfair. They had time for these things, she didn't. Furthermore, her salary was just about exactly the same as Terri's despite the fact that she had considerably more experience, and it was lower than Anna's, although she could accept that up to a point. Marybeth stated that she expected at least a 9 percent salary increase to make up for all the past inequities and to recognize the stress under which she worked. If she didn't receive this or at least something comparable, she would be forced to file a grievance with the personnel department.

21

LET'S GIVE HER A TRY; IT MAY WORK OUT

Sharon Murphy, the library's assistant director for administration and personnel, picked up the phone to call the university's personnel office and asked immediately to speak to Teresa Gonzales, head of staff employment. The two women knew each other well, and had interacted on many occasions. "Teresa," Sharon began, "the director and I have just finished interviewing Suzanne Forbush for the clerk-typist job in our administrative offices, and we're both puzzled. The position, as you know, is just a junior position working in the administrative offices. It involves a lot of report and memorandum typing, some work with data-entry equipment, and quite a lot of telephone answering. We were assuming you would send us a young person just starting out, with the personality to fit in well with an office staff in which everybody backstops everybody else. Teamwork is very important here.

"Suzanne has been working in the purchasing department for over five years, and most of her typing and data entry involved purchasing forms and not correspondence or reports. The performance evaluations in her file are not all that great, and she really expressed no particular interest in the library. For her it's just a job. I asked her why she had applied for this transfer, and she said to talk to you. So that's what I am doing. Frankly, we were not particularly impressed with her attitude, either."

"I was going to call you this afternoon, anyway," Teresa Gonzales said, "to brief you on this interview, but I got tied up with a federal statistical report we're compiling. As you noted, she's worked in purchasing for five years. She hasn't gotten on well over there, and last month they put her on terminal notice, which is the last step before firing her. Suzanne countered that by coming here and telling us that she was being fired because she had turned down her boss's sexual advances. I need not tell you that he completely denies this, and at this point we just have the two statements. However, Suzanne also wrote a letter to President Graubart, and Graubart told us he wanted to avoid a lawsuit that could be messy, because she told him, and for that matter me, that she would certainly sue if she was fired.

"It was Graubart who suggested we find a place to transfer her if possible, but sending her to you was, to be honest, my idea. She may work out just fine, or she may be the kind of employee who really ought to be fired. Purchasing said she was sloppy, inattentive, and rude to the vendors, and some of that is documented in performance evaluations, but there is no supporting evidence and Suzanne denies the whole thing. Sharon wanted to interject her reactions to this strategy, but she sensed that Teresa had more to say. She decided to hold her tongue for the moment and Teresa continued.

"The reason I thought the library administration office might be a good spot for her is because your office is composed totally of females, and it is the only place in the whole university that meets that description and has a job available. Look, we have to try and do what Graubart wants. Take her, and evaluate her work closely. If she doesn't work out, you have my assurance that we'll back you all the way on terminating her. And this time she certainly wouldn't be able to claim sexual harassment. If *that* was sexual harassment, and she really is a good worker, you'll be able to tell soon enough. If she is really as bad as purchasing says she is, you'll know that pretty quickly, too. We'll really appreciate your help with this one, because if we don't go through this process things might be legally sticky."

22

GO, TEAM, GO!

When Lawrence Huckaby first heard about it, he was amused. Some students would pull just about anything. Lawrence was library director at the state university, and while the university library was the source of some pride, it could not measure up to the excitement generated by the football team. The university always had a strong and fervently supported football team, and rivalries with other major state universities were heated.

It therefore did not surprise Lawrence that the undergraduate students who worked as clerical assistants in the main library were representative of the general fervor that football season always brought. Students performed a variety of support tasks, including the packaging and mailing of interlibrary loan shipments, using the addresses provided in the requests. Not surprisingly, many of these shipments went to universities that were heated football rivals. Sports rivalries were one thing, but they did not prevent academic libraries from cooperating and sharing resources. Nevertheless, Lawrence (and sometimes the others) was not above doing a little gloating at ALA meetings.

This was a little different, and Lawrence would probably never have known about it if he hadn't gotten the phone call from Betty Wishniak, who was library director at the state university across the river. Betty thought it was funny, too, as she made clear when she told him that in addition to interlibrary loan materials his library was also mailing "inspirational messages." It was obvious that he had not known about this, as she had suspected. "Whoever is putting these journal articles and books in the mail is also including little slips of paper with such comments as 'We'll kill the Wildcats' or 'The Wildcats have no chance.' You might want to look into it, Larry. Whoever is doing it may be doing it with other shipments, and not everybody has a sense of humor."

Lawrence did look into it, and it was not hard to find out what was happening. One of the student assistants, overcome with school spirit, had typed and duplicated little messages appropriate for each of the other nine universities in the conference. He was routinely enclosing a slip whenever a pack went to one of the schools. He grinned sheepishly (and rather charmingly, Lawrence thought) when he was confronted. He admitted what he had done, thought it did no harm and that, indeed, helped school spirit. Lawrence wasn't so sure, and pointed out that not everybody had a sense of humor. He told the student assistant to stop, and the student said he would. Lawrence went back to his office and forgot about it.

It was too late, for it became obvious in the next two days that there were at least three people who did not share his and Betty Wishniak's sense of humor. These included the librarian at Transprairie State (perhaps because they hardly ever won a football game), the university president to whom she reported the incident, and the president of Lawrence's own university (although he already knew President Grubble had no sense of humor), whom the president of Transprairie had called. President Grubble was not amused, was not pleased that Librarian Huckaby took the issue so lightly, and was not reassured to learn that the student had been identified and reprimanded and had agreed to stop. That was not enough for President Grubble. He wanted Lawrence to tell him the name of the student and turn the issue over to the dean of students for disciplinary action. It was clear that for Grubble the appropriate disciplinary action was expulsion from the university.

23

PLEASE DON'T LET MY MARRIAGE BE DESTROYED!

As director of a major public library system with forty branches and several hundred employees, Allan Mosbach could not be expected to know all his employees, particularly the clerical ones. If he recalled Marcia Harrison at all, it was vaguely as a young woman who worked in the printing and duplicating area, although there were several such young women in that group. He did know Warren Brinson, her supervisor. Warren was not a librarian, as indeed there was no need for a supervisor of printing and duplicating to be a librarian. He had come to the library about four years ago, and his performance evaluations had been positive. He reported through a management chain to the assistant director for administration. Whenever Allan needed printing or duplicating work in which he was personally involved and interested, it had been prepared correctly and on time.

All of which made the letter on his desk particularly disturbing. It was from a Rodney Harrison, whom he did not know at all but who identified himself as the husband of Marcia Harrison. The letter was long, impassioned, and not always correct from a grammatic and spelling standpoint, but the message was clear. It had arrived in the mail this morning, addressed to him and marked *personal and confidential.* As she had been instructed, Allan's secretary brought such mail to him unopened. As he reread the letter, Allan knew that he was the only one in the library who knew of its contents.

In the letter was an anguished plea for help from Rodney Harrison. His wife, Marcia, was having an affair with her supervisor, Warren Brinson, and this had been going on for six months. She had initially denied the affair, but finally confessed it to him. According to Harrison's letter, Marcia wanted to break off the affair but did not have the strength to do so. Harrison felt that Warren Brinson had some sort of power over his wife and would not let her go.

Harrison did not ask that the library fire Brinson, or for that matter fire his wife. He asked rather that the library director do something to separate them from daily contact. It was a large library, he pointed out, with many jobs and many branches in the county. If his wife could only be removed from daily contact with her supervisor, he was quite certain that the affair would end. Indeed, Marcia had told him that without daily involvement with her supervisor she would be able to do what she really wanted to do, which was break off the relationship.

Harrison concluded his emotional letter by stating that he considered Mr. Mosbach the last hope for saving this marriage, and that he was not asking this only for himself and for his wife, who was too embarrassed to bring the issue to him, but that he was making this plea also on behalf of their two small children.

24

THE DRINKING EMPLOYEE

Annabelle Bowrey was library director at Oakwood University, and had been for twelve years. Oakwood was a good place in which to work, a major research university without the pretentions of cracking the Top Ten. There were the usual problems of inadequate funding for everything, including the library, but in general Annabelle was satisfied. Relations with the administration and the faculty were at least civil, and she was genuinely pleased with the staff she had acquired and trained. With fifty professionals and over one hundred other permanent staff members, she could not keep track of everyone on a continuing basis, but she thought she knew all of her people well enough so that they would come to her if they had concerns and problems. And indeed they had treated her as a friend.

Annabelle had become increasingly aware of the fact that she hadn't seem much of Beulah Morton lately, and at first she simply dismissed it as coincidence. Beulah was in charge of interlibrary loan services, which was located in another part of the library building. Interlibrary loan, which reported through Frances Watanabe, head of reference, to Walter Jankowski, assistant director for public services, had the usual problems of heavy workloads and substantial backlogs, but nothing special. And yet Annabelle had not noticed Beulah at any of the last three monthly professional staff meetings, although Annabelle couldn't swear that Beulah hadn't been there. She had even asked Marlys Kraus, who as personnel officer had the office next to hers, if there was anything unusual about Beulah. Marlys had looked surprised, said, no, not to her knowledge, and asked what Annabelle had in mind. Annabelle decided to drop the issue. Perhaps it was coincidence, and in any case there were no operational problems here to concern her.

Nevertheless, the issue continued to nag at her. Once she had called Beulah, figuring that she'd think of a question when she got her on the phone, only to be told that Beulah had left for the afternoon for a dental appointment. A week latter she "casually" dropped by, only to be told that she had just missed Mrs. Morton, who had left for a committee meeting at the state library.

Annabelle was not good at playing games, and decided to talk to

Walter Jankowski directly. "Wally," she began immediately, "is there anything about Beulah Morton that I don't know but perhaps *should* know?"

"Why do you ask?" Walter parried.

"Because I never seem to see her. If something is going on I think you'd better tell me."

Walter sighed. "Shut the door and sit down. Beulah's marriage of twenty-five years split up six months ago. She's taking it pretty hard, and I'm afraid she has found escape through drinking. We all thought she'd be over it by now, but it's taken longer than we thought. If you haven't seen Beulah it's because we haven't seen much of her, either."

Annabelle was both incredulous and angry. "This has been going on for six months?" she demanded to know.

"Actually, closer to about four months," Walter Jankowski responded like a little boy with his hand caught in the cookie jar.

Annabelle was not dissuaded. "Four months! Who else knows about this besides you and now me?"

"Actually, a lot of people know. Beulah's staff knows. Frances Watanabe and I know. Maybe a couple of others. Okay, maybe we were wrong. All right, we *were* wrong. But we all know Beulah, and we know she got a bum deal when her husband walked out. We were covering for her because we were trying to help her overcome the initial shock. We didn't know it would go on this long."

25 VEHICLE SAFETY AND INDIVIDUAL RIGHTS

Gloria Branscomb had agreed enthusiastically when the chief of police asked if the library would be willing to participate in the campaign for traffic safety. It was an important and useful public service, and certainly not controversial. The library reached a whole range of people, but particularly young people, whose involvement ranged from their roles as pedestrians to bicycle riders to new drivers. Rules of road and traffic safety, reminders about the use of seat belts, about driving while intoxicated, about wearing reflecting colors on bicycles and facing the traffic while walking—all of these injunctions had been stressed and well received.

There had been programs in the library auditorium in which police and safety experts had spoken. There had been lighter approaches, including games and contests and a safety quiz with prizes for students of all ages. Both the newspaper and the local TV station had given the campaign, and the library, a good deal of very positive publicity. Gloria was pleased, the library board was pleased, the mayor was pleased, the chief of police was pleased. It was a well-planned, well-executed campaign, and it would continue.

Unfortunately all this general euphoria and good will was too good to last. Henrietta Overmeyer, president of the garden club, wife of the bank president, and a major factor in just about every civic organization, was not in any sense a mean or evil person. Indeed, in her own pompous way she was a strong supporter of the library and its programs. It was just that she was so overbearing—yes, pompous *was* the right word—whatever she said came out as a command.

It was Henrietta Overmeyer who had just wandered into the director's office one day; typically, she never made appointments but simply swept in like the tide. "Gloria," she began sweetly. "I think it is just wonderful what you people are doing to help promote traffic safety. But isn't it a bit odd that one of your own children's librarians, with such an opportunity to be a wonderful role model, provides such an unfortunate example?" Gloria looked puzzled. "But, my dear, surely you know I'm talking about Jeff Meyer, who rides that dreadfully noisy Kawasaki motorcycle and doesn't even wear a helmet?"

Of course Gloria knew Jeff Meyer. Male children's librarians were rare, but Jeff was very good, very dedicated, and very much a favorite with the patrons in the children's and young adult's room. He was hardly stereotypical, and that certainly pleased Gloria although she knew it wasn't supposed to matter. He was about 27, tall, blond, and athletic; he had formed a special bond with the kids and never talked down to them. Gloria was pretty sure that at least part of the strong junior high female attendance in the library came from girls with a crush on Jeff, and she wasn't sure that didn't also apply to some of the adult staff members. In any case, Jeff was a solid and well-trained librarian, and she was delighted to have him. She knew he rode a Kawasaki, and that was part of his non-stereotypical charm. She didn't know that he didn't wear a helmet when he rode it.

She decided to talk to Jeff. He was, as always, polite and calm, but also surprisingly stubborn. He did not wear a helmet because he didn't believe all of those reports that suggested they were necessary. He was a careful rider who had never had an accident, and he enjoyed riding bareheaded. Wearing a helmet was not required by law, and he suggested that Mrs. Overmeyer should mind her own business.

26

A POTENTIAL CONFLICT OF VIEWPOINTS—1

This is the day for the annual performance review for Reference Librarian Antoinette (Toni) Dvorak. The interview, as in the past two years, will be conducted by Head of Reference Francine Thayer. As is normal at Midstate University libraries, Francine has made herself some notes concerning issues to be discussed. After the meeting, which normally takes between thirty minutes and an hour, Francine is responsible for writing up the results of the discussion, including both the points she has raised and the issues raised by Toni, and concluding with some sort of overall evaluation. That evaluation not only becomes a part of the tenure dossier, but also serves as a basis for the awarding of merit salary increases to take effect on July 1, three months from now.

As she awaits Toni's arrival in her office, Francine's orderly mind reviews the facts in this case and the points she plans to make during the discussion. Toni was hired three years ago, after receiving her M.L.S. degree, as an assistant librarian in the reference department, and has been in this post since her date of employment. She has now spent three years on the tenure track, and a tenure decision (retention on a permanent basis with promotion to associate librarian, or termination at the end of the seventh year) must be made by the end of the sixth year of service. That recommendation, initially made by the head of reference, will be reviewed by the assistant director for pubic services, the library's advisory committee on promotion and tenure, and the library director. Ultimately it must be approved by the president and transmitted to the board of trustees, but approval at that level is pro forma as long as all evaluations up to that point are positive. There are also provisions for termination at any point along the tenure process, but these provisions are employed only in drastic cases.

Francine sees no reason for such action in Toni's case, but she is nevertheless concerned about what she perceives as a lack of adequate progress toward the tenure decision that must be made in three years; she plans to discuss these issues seriously and frankly with Toni. Antoinette Dvorak is one of eight professional reference librarians in the department. Five are already tenured, and the others are on the tenure track. The reference staff has the responsibility for the main library reference desk on a rotating basis, with two on duty at any given time. Individuals handle in-person and telephonic reference inquiries while on the desk, and undertake longer searches and bibliographies during the approximately half-time they have no desk duties. A combination of manual and machine tools are used, and reference librarians are given a great deal of latitude in determining the approach to be used.

Librarians on the tenure track are not specifically required to undertake research and publication, although that is encouraged. They are judged by a combination of factors, including quality of service as documented by users' unsolicited comments and letters; service to the university, the library, and the profession; the observations of the supervisor; and evidence of professional growth, particularly in the absence of significant research publication.

In Francine's view, Toni Dvorak's performance has been adequate but not particularly praiseworthy, and as a result her salary increases have been average. Her file contains no record of comments from library users, either faculty or students, of a positive or negative nature. What is particularly disturbing to Francine is her perception of a total lack of professional growth and development. There has not only been no research and no publication, but also no professional involvement of any sort. Toni comes to work and does her job adequately, but that is about all. This sort of situation, if continued, will seriously endanger if not completely destroy her chances for a positive tenure decision three years from now. Francine knows that Toni lives in an apartment with her mother, and that this elderly lady has been in ill health for quite some time, although Toni keeps to herself and does not discuss her private problems. Nevertheless, Francine surmises that this may be a reason for the lack of growth and development, about which Francine is very disappointed because Toni Dvorak had shown much promise in her schoolwork and her interviews. The first two performance reviews were rather routine, and did not include any sort of threat to the achievement of tenure. Francine feels that this is the time to stop pulling punches, for the sake of the department but most particularly for Toni's sake.

Toni Dvorak is not really looking forward to this review session, which, like the last two, she thinks will be rather routine and a waste of time. The last three years, she reflects, have been an incredible continuation of job pressures that barely allowed her to think, let along plan what to do next. The reference department is understaffed by about four reference librarians, and as a result work is constantly backed up. Francine is a nice enough person, but not a particularly effective supervisor in protecting her people. If she were, she would have demanded some level of balance between staffing and workload. Salary increases for the library as a whole have barely kept up with the cost of living, and after three years Toni has the sense that she has made no progress at all. Her own salary increases, she knows, have been smaller than those received by some of her colleagues, although that issue is never discussed openly. She doubts that Francine knows how hard they all work—how hard she works. Her mother has been ill for several years, and since Toni is her only support and lives with her, Toni has little peace and relaxation when she gets home. She knows that the library at least theoretically expects some level of professional participation and growth from her besides her work time, but that expectation is a joke! Available travel funds don't even remotely cover the cost of conference attendance, and she would have the additional problem of arranging care for her mother. That's why she doesn't serve on committees—committees mean work for which she has no time, and meetings for which she has no money. Toni is not looking forward to this meeting because she doubts that Francine really understands or cares. However, these annual sessions are required even if they don't mean anything, so she just wants to get it over with.

27 A POTENTIAL CONFLICT OF VIEWPOINTS—2

The Metropolis City Public Library has a central cataloging department consisting of the department manager, five professional catalogers, and clerical support. Today is the annual performance review for cataloger Deborah Grimsley, and as usual it will be conducted by cataloging department head Marie Schultz. As Marie prepares for this meeting, she is pleased in the feeling that hers is a smoothly operating process, and she is willing to take credit for both her leadership and her talent in selecting the catalogers who work for her. Backlogs do exist but they are not nearly as large as in similar public library systems; and overall morale in the cataloging department and cooperation with the rest of the library are good. Like many libraries, Metropolis is moving toward an increase in networking and resource sharing, as well as cooperative cataloging, and the staff has handled all of this well. The professional staff is part of a municipal union, and salary increases are negotiated as part of the contract. This provides no opportunity for merit increases, but all employees know this when they accept their positions. The salaries negotiated for librarians have not been too bad, when compared to reports from similar public libraries. There is, of course, opportunity for promotional salary increases whenever promotions occur.

It is just this possibility that Marie wants to discuss with Debbie Grimsley, and she is pleased at the prospect. Debbie is her best cataloger. She has told her this before, and she will tell her again today. What makes this particularly remarkable is that Debbie is only five years out of library school, and came to Metropolis City right after completing her degree. What Debbie does not know, because at this point nobody except the director knows, is that Marie will be relocating to Arizona in three months because of her husband's medical condition. Marie wants to assure a successful continuation of the present operation, and Debbie Grimsley is the best choice to succeed her. When she made this suggestion to the library director she appeared receptive and urged Marie to sound out her candidate as to her willingness to accept the post, prior to making a recommendation.

As Marie reviews the options, her conclusions are reinforced. Debbie Grimsley is the best cataloger, and although she is not the most senior, promotions do not have to be based on seniority. In any case, her fellow workers like and respect her, and will raise no difficulty. Her job, she is sure Debbie realizes but is going to stress, is considerably different from Debbie's. It really allows very little time for cataloging, because it requires attendance at regional and state planning meetings, as well as professional activity at the national level. She knows that Debbie is modest and self-effacing and may argue that she is not ready for such a promotional assignment. However, Marie is quite confident that Debbie is ready. She knows the work and she is good with people. The job provides an immediate salary increase of $6,000 a year and a transfer to management in which greater future salary increases and promotions are possible. This is Debbie's best chance to grow and progress, and Marie is going to do her best to persuade Debbie to accept this opportunity. Marie is looking forward to this meeting.

As Debbie approaches the annual performance review, she has neither concerns nor particular expectations. Her feelings run as follows:

> I think I am doing good work; indeed, Marie has told me so on a number of occasions. What I like best about my job is that it allows me the freedom to operate without unnecessary interference. Although this is my first professional job, I gather that other librarians and some other catalogers are not as fortunate. I guess I really don't have a great deal of ambition because I'm happy where I am and in what I'm doing, and my job allows me to be fully involved in local environmental groups, and there is plenty that needs to be done there. I also enjoy concerts and theaters, and so I have something of the best of all worlds. The salary isn't all that great but my living style is modest and I can live with it. Besides, it *is* part of the union contract negotiation, so there's no point in worrying about it.
>
> Marie and I have had these annual review sessions three times in the past, and they've all been pleasant and rather brief. I imagine this one will be too, and because praise is always nice to receive, I'm looking forward to it.

28

THE CHILDREN'S ROOM FOR STAFF BABYSITTING

Nicole Deveraux was prompt for her 2:00 appointment with Public Library Director Frank Wittington. Indeed, she might have been early, because she was already waiting in his outer office when he returned from his Kiwanis luncheon at 1:55. Frank was always pleased to talk to Nicole, who had been head of the children's department for the last four years and was an excellent administrator and innovator. The department had a fine reputation in the community, and Nicole and he had established a warm and casual relationship. He was therefore surprised when she had called him at home to request this appointment, and he feared that she might have come to tell him about an outside job offer. If so, he certainly planned to do what he could to keep her.

Nicole seemed nervous when he asked her to follow him into his office, and she made a point of shutting the door immediately while he hung up his coat. All of this seemed to confirm his suspicions. But he was wrong. Nicole began right away: "I'm sorry to have called you at home to set up this appointment, but if I had scheduled it through Nancy she would have wanted to know what it was about, and I didn't want to lie. I specifically waited until yesterday evening because I know that Nancy is off today. I appreciate your seeing me on such short notice."

Frank was puzzled. Nancy Barrington was his personal secretary, and had been for the last two years. A divorced mother of two preschool children, Nancy had overcome a good deal of difficulty to make something of herself, particularly after her ex-husband had left her and ultimately disappeared, making the court-ordered child support payments something of a joke. Nancy never complained about her difficulties, and she was an excellent secretary. She also appeared to get along well with all of the library staff members, including Nicole. He was particularly surprised as Nicole and Nancy were both black, and were probably the two most visible minority staff members in a largely white staff in this midwestern city. They were not personal friends, but that was not unexpected. Nicole had come to the United States from Haiti as a small child, the daughter of a professor; her circle of friends was not the same as Nancy's, who had literally pulled herself out of the ghetto by sheer willpower and effort.

"I don't understand. What has Nancy to do with this?" Frank asked.

"Let me start at the beginning," Nicole responded. "About six months ago Nancy came into the children's room one morning with her children. The boy is about 2½, the girl about 3½. She explained that her babysitter had suddenly become ill, and she didn't have time to find a replacement on such short notice. I agreed that we could help out in such an emergency, and there was no problem. The children are really too young to spend that much time in a library children's room, and although they are both well behaved you can understand that they require special care and special attention from the staff. Nancy came down on both her breaks and on her lunch hour to feed them and spend some time with them. I had a meeting that afternoon, and the two kids napped in my office. Nancy picked them up at 5:00, expressed her appreciation, and took them home."

"Well, emergencies do happen,' Frank commented. "It was nice of you to help her out, but why are you mentioning this now?"

"I'm bringing it up because it has happened four times since then. The average seems to be about once a month. Each time Nancy just appears with the children, apologizes for the emergency, and asks if we can help. Last month, at Christmas, she gave me a rather expensive present, far more expensive than any casual relationship might warrant, and insisted I keep it because she was so grateful. I'm concerned that Nancy is just assuming that this is a logical backstop arrangement for whenever something goes wrong. Has she ever mentioned any of this to you, Frank?" Frank shook his head.

"I thought not, and that's why I wanted to speak to you. This is a bad idea and it establishes a bad precedent. We have too many other things to do, and we're not geared for this. Even with Nancy coming down several times a day, it places a tremendous responsibility not just on me but also on the rest of the children's room staff. None of them has said anything to me about it, but I think they have talked about it to each other. Some of the adult patrons have started to notice, too. Fortunately, or perhaps unfortunately, they probably think the children are mine."

Nicole's smile broke the tension that Frank had started to feel. At least she still had a sense of humor about this. Nevertheless, it was a problem, and Nicole quite correctly expected him to deal with it. He felt a moment of annoyance with Nancy for never having brought the issue to his attention herself, but then he realized that he would have had very little advice to offer and that Nancy probably knew that. Neither the library nor the municipal government had any sort of arrangement for child care. Some communities did, but not this conservative midwestern town. It occurred to him that Nancy, used to having to cope with her own problems and her own emergencies, had simply improvised as well as she could. About whether or not she felt that Nicole, as a fellow black, owed her particular help or allegiance, he preferred not to speculate.

29

A REQUEST FOR TRANSFER

Public library personnel director Sharon McCorkle had never seen Rebecca Bartram look or act so animated. The first words that came to mind when thinking about Becky Bartram might be quiet, shy, withdrawn, even mousy, unkind as that last adjective was. In the five years that Becky had worked at Millerton since coming here as a cataloger, Sharon could not recall a single conversation that wasn't perfunctory or superficial. That Becky was shy and lacked social graces, and had never learned to wear clothes or makeup to enhance what could really be a pretty face, was not crucial to her work as a cataloger. She was solid and dependable if unspectacular, but Sharon and Becky's supervisor had decided some time ago that while Becky's work was satisfactory, there was no potential for promotion to a management post. As Becky seemed satisfied with this arrangement (it occurred to Sharon that she really knew nothing about Becky's outside interests and what she did in her spare time) there appeared to be no need to fix what wasn't broken.

Rebecca Bartram's request (almost demand) for this appointment had been the first surprise; her agitation was the second. "What can I do for you, Becky?" Sharon began.

"Gee, I'm surprised you haven't already guessed, Ms. McCorkle. I've just learned that Hannah Morgenstern is moving out west with her husband, and that opens up the genealogy librarian position. That's what I'm here to talk about." Becky actually smiled!

"Are you interested in applying for the position?" Sharon asked.

Becky's smile turned into a puzzled frown. "Well, of course. I'm absolutely perfect for the job. I would have mentioned it earlier, but I had no reason to think that Hannah would ever leave. As you know, my undergraduate major was in history, and I've been taking courses toward the master's at the university. Genealogy is my great area of interest! I work on it in my spare time."

Sharon now recalled the bachelor's in history, but that wasn't unusual for library science students. She didn't know about either the advanced courses or the fascination with local history. She decided to proceed cautiously, because it was necessary to calm down Becky's almost childlike enthusiasm. "A knowledge of history and genealogy is obviously important, but there are other factors that will have to go into the decision of whom to appoint. Personality factors are very important. The genealogy librarian works directly with patrons, some of whom can be very difficult to deal with. It requires tact; it requires an ability to plan and prioritize."

Becky was barely listening. She asked Sharon, "What do I need to do to apply?"

"The procedure is exactly the same as for an initial hiring. You need to fill out the application form, although we already have your résumé and other information. You do understand that this will be a full and open search, including advertisements and perhaps outside candidates?"

"Oh, sure, I understand you have to go through all the procedures," was Becky's only reaction. She took the proffered application form and practically skipped out of the office. Sharon watched her leave, and shook her head sadly. Appointing Becky Bartram as genealogy librarian was impossible! But how do we tell her?

30

INTELLECTUAL MOONLIGHTING ON LIBRARY TIME?

University library director Wilfred Batchelor found the campus mail envelope in his mail tray surprising, both because it was marked *strictly personal* and because it bore no return address. It could have come from anyone in the university, or for that matter from an outsider with access to any departmental mail bin. As she had been instructed in such cases, Wil's secretary had not opened the envelope, although normally she opened his mail and arranged it for him together with appropriate background correspondence. When he opened the envelope there was no letter or note, only a photocopy of a magazine page.

It was a book review from one of the children's literature review journals, a review of a book of children's stories unique to the settlement of the American West. These were the stories about animals, Indians, and the early settlers that parents apparently told their children. Whoever had sent him the review (which by the way was quite positive) had realized that as a university library director he was not likely to keep up with children's literature and had wanted specifically for him to see this review. But why?

He began to read the review again, and suddenly it made sense. The book's author, Ainsley Parrish, was quite obviously none other than Roger A. Parrish. Roger Parrish was the library's humanities bibliographer, a tenured associate librarian. Batchelor recalled that Parrish had a master's degree in history, and that the early West was his area of specialization. There could be no doubt that this was the same person.

But if so, why had Roger never mentioned this? It might or might not qualify as research, but it probably would, and it could be helpful in making a case for promotion to full librarian. Why the secrecy?

And suddenly it all began to make sense. Wilfred recalled the fact that Roger was almost never in his office when you called him, and that on two occasions when it was necessary to look for him he could not be located. His explanations for those absences had seemed plausible, and there had been no reason to question them. His continual absence from his office when called could have been coincidence. Humanities bibliographers obviously spend a great deal of time in the stacks and in the offices of history professors. Nobody at this library was expected to account for every minute of his or her time or to present a time card.

Nevertheless, Wilfred Batchelor was now suspicious. Why would he have kept so quiet about this book unless . . . ? Unless he were writing most or all of it on library time! And why would a scholar have written under what could be an attempt to hide his identity? The university had no fixed written policy about the mixture of outside activities and university activities, and the library had no stated policy either, except for the understanding that all assigned duties had to be performed. Were they being performed? How did one monitor the work of the humanities bibliographer, who certainly seemed on good terms with the history faculty members? Whoever had sent this to him anonymously had meant to convey a message, and although he despised anonymous messages he wasn't sure he could ignore this one. Should he speak to Roger directly? Should he speak to Lucille Miller, the assistant director for public services to whom Roger nominally reported?

31

A CONCERN ABOUT POSSIBLE NEPOTISM

Library director Amanda Byrd looked over the final report of the search and screen committee for the post of assistant director for technical services, a position vacated by the retirement of Harold Goldman, and she felt comfortable with the recommendations. The committee, as a normal part of university faculty searches, had winnowed down a list of eighteen initial candidates to four persons who were brought in for interviews; they recommended two names as acceptable, without ranking them. Amanda felt comfortable with either of the two.

The outside candidate, Jacqueline Eastbrook, was currently filling the same position in a smaller university. Her recommendations had been enthusiastically positive, and she had made a fine impression during the interview process. Amanda Byrd felt quite certain that the staff would have no objection if she were selected. A woman not yet 40 and definitely a comer within the profession, Jackie Eastbrook had a reputation as a problem solver. She had cleared up processing backlogs at Southwestern State, she had supervised the implementation of new hardware and software systems, and she served on a number of ALA committees concerned with technical services. Her emergence during the search process had been an unexpected bonus.

However, the sentimental choice, for both the staff and, in truth, for Amanda, was still Sue Haddock, the head of cataloging. Sue had been with the library for twenty-four years. She had risen through the ranks from junior cataloger to her present post, where she had been for eight years. Always gracious and well liked, Sue had served on a number of library-wide and university-wide committees, and had earned the respect not only of her colleagues but also of faculty and administrators. Not as well known nationally as Jackie Eastbrook and probably not as flashy, Sue had nevertheless "paid her dues." Amanda was certain that most of the staff considered the search process a formality and expected Sue to be promoted, although that preconception did not preclude a very positive reaction to Jackie Eastbrook. The other candidates did not really compare, and Amanda thought the committee correct in eliminating them. Sue, in her typically quiet and unassuming yet efficient way, had never spoken directly to Amanda about any sort of claim on the position. She had followed the normal search procedures, and yet Amanda was quite sure she expected this promotion.

Promoting Sue Haddock was probably the easier decision, certainly the more popular one and plausibly even the best one. However, there was one complication, and it had not occurred to anyone up until this time. Sue's daughter Linda had been hired as an assistant librarian for the serials department upon graduation from library school two years ago. There was nothing wrong with that process; Linda had high grades, strong letters of recommendation, and she had impressed the search committee. Sue had never sought to intercede on behalf of her daughter. However, she continued to live at home with her parents, and mother and daughter usually came to work together.

If Sue Haddock were promoted to the post of assistant director for technical services, her daughter would be working for her, although through an intermediate supervisor. The serials department was a part of technical services.

32

AN AIDS CASE ON THE LIBRARY STAFF

Library director Celeste Turnbull was a little surprised that Cindy Handlin had scheduled a formal appointment for 10:00 this morning. The New Saxony County Public Library was an informal place, with seven professional librarians and a full-time support staff of thirteen and other assorted part-timers, volunteers, and students. Celeste's door was usually open, and people just dropped in. Celeste had made it a point to get to know all the staff quite well, and she was generally pleased. She was particularly happy about Cindy, who had joined the library staff straight out of library school eight months ago as assistant children's librarian. Cindy, who was young and refreshing, had a particularly strong rapport with the preschoolers who came to the library. They looked on her as a trusted friend, and not as an adult authority figure. Rachel Robertson, the head of the children's library department, had commented to Celeste on a number of occasions how pleased she was that they had selected Cindy. They all felt a little lucky, too. Hannover, the county seat, and the rest of New Saxony County were not exactly hotbeds of cultural and social activity, and it was not easy to recruit bright young librarians who were not already committed to the area. As the names suggested, this part of the country had been settled by German immigrant farmers. They were good solid people, with a genuine warmth. They were also deeply religious and politically conservative, and the standing joke was that the big social event occurred each Saturday morning when the farm pickup trucks pulled into the K-Mart. There were local clubs, but no real culture nearer than River Falls, fifty miles away, because the one local college was a small fundamentalist school that kept to itself. Any concern about how Cindy might fit in at the library, however, had long ago been forgotten. She was popular with what eligible local professional young men there were, and she had frequent dinner invitations to the homes of other staff members. Most of all, however, Cindy had a commitment to children's service in the library, and to children's literature. It had all worked out beautifully.

Celeste was surprised when Cindy closed the office door behind her and did not return Celeste's smile of welcome. Cindy sat down and immediately started to speak. "Celeste, I just found out I have AIDS," she said simply.

Celeste took a moment to absorb this momentous news, then swallowed and said, "Cindy, how could this have happened?" The moment the words had escaped her lips, Celeste regretted them. She said, "I'm sorry, I had no right to ask you that."

Cindy allowed herself a wan little smile. "That's all right, I have to get used to the question. It's the first one my mother asked, and I'm sure others will ask it later. I really don't know. I've never used drugs, and I haven't had any blood transfusions. I wish I had, because people accept that explanation more easily. I've been feeling basically okay, but occasionally nauseated. So I went to see the doctor, expecting some medication for an upset stomach. It was he who dropped this two-ton weight on my head. At this point he, my parents, and now you are the only ones who know."

Cindy took a sip from the cup of coffee she had brought with her, and went on. "I've been trying to wrack my brain about how this happened, and I just don't know. I'm not a promiscuous person, although some people in this community might think so. I dated fairly regularly while in college and in library school. Noting really serious or permanent. It could perhaps be one of five or six guys, but by now I've lost touch with all of them. I'm not really sure I want to know, and I'm not certain it really matters at this point. Does it?"

Celeste tried to be reassuring and supportive. "No, of course it doesn't. The important thing is that you *are* feeling okay right now, and you could for a long time to come. They're working very hard on cures, and they've already made a great deal of progress in slowing the disease."

Celeste did not ask the next question, but Cindy anticipated it. "There is really no way to tell how rapidly this illness might or might not develop. The doctor told me there is no way to predict. I might show no outward symptoms for months or even years, or I might go downhill pretty fast. The only thing I'm sure of is that I have it."

The conversation continued, a little awkwardly, for a while longer, and then Cindy came to her point. "I came to tell you, Celeste, because I thought you should know. I didn't have to tell you, at least not yet. I want you to promise me that you will mention this to nobody else, at least until I say you can."

Celeste paused a long time before answering. "I'm not sure I can make that promise, Cindy. There may be county rules that apply, and I will have to check out discreetly what these might be. I think that one of us, probably you, should also tell Rachel. I'm sure you will find her supportive and understanding. Finally, I have to worry about the library, the children, and the parents who have entrusted them to us. We know a great deal about how AIDS is not communicated, and while there is still some hysteria, I think the paranoia of the Ryan White case is behind us. However, AIDS is still an infectious and communicable disease. I know that you would never consciously let any of the children drink from your cup, but how could you be sure they wouldn't while you weren't watching? I'm not even sure that matters. I'm not certain *what* I know at this point, but there are some things I need to find out and think about. County policies, for one. I would like to talk to your doctor if you will permit me. I don't know if I can make the promises you've asked me to make. The one thing I will promise is that I won't do anything further without first talking to you again."

II

INTERACTIONS WITH SUPERIORS

THE COMMUNITY ROOM

Peter Campanis, library director, and Lyle Pocklington, chairman of the board of trustees, had been an excellent team for the last ten years, by coincidence having taken up their posts at the Central City Public Library at the same time. Between them there was a bond of mutual respect and trust. Peter was an excellent librarian and administrator. Lyle, as president of the largest local bank, was an astute businessman, who understood how to get things done. They shared a vision of a better Central City Public Library. It was Lyle who had suggested, when the architectural plans for the present main library building were being drawn up six years ago, that the library should have a large community room. That room, with movable partitions, could be used for several small meetings, or even one large one seating as many as 200 people in folding chairs. When Peter had pointed out that the library rarely had either internal or external need for such a large room, it was Lyle who had shown him that Central City lacked adequate meeting space for community groups. Having such space available would tie these groups to the library, create instant political support, and serve the needs of the community.

Lyle, as in so many things, had been correct. The community room had been an instant success. The policies drawn up by Peter and approved by the board were simple and easy to enforce. The room was available on a reserved first-come-first-served basis to any not-for-profit community groups, provided that the group in its activities broke no laws or local regulations, that no food or beverages were served, and that the room would be returned to its original state before it was vacated. The policy was intentionally broad and inclusive to be consistent with the ALA Library Bill of Rights and legal rulings. Scheduling of the room was coordinated by Peter's secretary, and there had been no problems. There were groups with diverse political solutions to problems in the Middle East; alcohol, drug, and diet support groups; travel clubs and musical groups (the room contained a piano). They all scheduled and used the room without difficulty, and the library had indeed benefited in visibility and support. Virtually all of the groups met in the evenings or on weekends, and Peter was rarely in the office on those occasions. He knew only vaguely about the groups using the facilities, and had attended only a couple of the travel and lecture programs.

Thus, he would have known little about the Magic Club, a group that started meeting in the community room once a month. Peter assumed that it was a group of amateur magicians sharing their tricks and putting on demonstrations. It was finally a letter to the editor of the local newspaper that alerted him. Written by the distraught mother of one of the individuals who belonged to the club, it charged that the "magic club" was really a group of high school and college students who met to explore and practice satanic rituals. Other letters followed, and finally the newspaper did a feature on the club (which had about twenty-five members) and printed an interview with a woman in another city who claimed that her son had committed suicide based on the practices of a similar group. The publicity that came to the library from this was anything but positive, and instead of dying down it seemed to be snowballing.

This was the subject of a phone call from Lyle Pocklington to Peter Campanis. They conversed often, over the telephone and over lunch, and had dinner at each other's houses on occasion, so the call itself was no surprise. The subject, however, was troubling. Since the board would be having its regular monthly meeting a week from Thursday, Lyle wanted to schedule a brief executive session before the regular agenda. He wanted Peter to draft the necessary revisions to the community room use policies that would allow them to get rid of this so-called Magic Club. Peter was genuinely troubled, and spent the next nine days in agonized analysis of his own feelings, as well as in review of appropriate ALA documents.

When Lyle convened the executive session, he told the board members that they already knew of the problems that had been caused by this group of young satanists, and that the board was here to amend the policies and return the room to its appropriate use. He then called on Peter for his recommended changes. Perter explained that he had no recommendations to make. While this use of the room was unfortunate, he considered it a totally appropriate expression of the right of free speech. To draft rigged rules specifically to deny access to this group would, in his judgment, amount to censorship. It would establish dangerous precedents.

Lyle, for the first time since Peter had known him, was genuinely angry and red in the face. "Don't give me lectures about censorship," he shouted. "I know what it is just as well as you do. When the people from the Eagle Alliance wanted us to remove the books of Kurt Vonnegut, *that* was censorship! When that black fundamentalist preacher wanted us to remove *Huckleberry Finn, that* was censorship! We all backed you on those issues 100 percent, and we won. And if necessary, we'll do it again whenever we have to. However, this stupid club doesn't raise any issues of censorship. They can meet *anywhere*, including the recreation rooms of the members' homes, if the parents are dumb enough to let them in! We've worked very hard together to build a strong library and community support. We've come a long way, but there is still a long road ahead. I don't have to remind you that in two years we'll be presenting the bond referendum for the two new branches. Are you willing to throw all that away for a bunch of self-indulgent and maybe dangerous kids who represent no issue except the gratification of that self-indulgence? I can't believe you would be that stupid and that irresponsible!"

With that, Lyle Pocklington slammed down his gavel, adjourning the executive session of the board.

34

THE HIGH AND HIDDEN COST OF COOPERATION

Polly Morton looked over her numbers one more time. They were rough estimates, but they were generally correct, she was quite sure. Polly was director of the Crossley College Library. Crossley was a fine, private, four-year liberal arts college located in the upper midwest. Originally church-founded, it had long since become essentially nondenominational; and the sharp reduction in church funding support also reflected the loosening of ties with the church over time, all by mutual consent. For quite a while Crossley, operating as an independent institution, had done just fine. Its reputation was good, the campus was beautiful, and the faculty was composed of caring teachers, even if they were not outstanding scholars. In the last decade things had gotten tougher for Crossley, as for many residential liberal arts colleges. Tuition was much higher than at state universities and municipal colleges, and because of the sparse population in the area in which it was located, Crossley had to depend on a national recruitment campaign. For a while there had also been a larger number of international students, particularly from the Middle East and Africa, but that had decreased, in part because of political developments in those areas and in part because Crossley winters were too cold and bleak for students not used to them.

Crossley did not have many distinguished and affluent alumni. The really prominent ones had graduate degrees from other institutions, and their loyalties were divided because they were expected to support the schools from which they had obtained their medical, law, or business administration degrees. In this last decade of tight budgets, with the prospects of more problems to come, Polly felt that the library had been treated as fairly as possible. The collection had historically been strong for a school of its size and aspirations, and there had been a strong campus commitment not to let it weaken. Still, they were living under tightened circumstances. Salaries were low, and the library staff had declined slightly through attrition. The delivery of every new computer terminal was cause for celebration.

It was in this context that Polly looked at her rough calculations concerning the cost of resource sharing. Crossley belonged to the statewide network that had been forged by the state library. One of the cornerstones of this effort was broadened access for interlibrary loans, and the state legislature had authorized, on a proposal from the state librarian, a subsidy to reimburse lenders $5 per transaction provided they enacted no other charges. Polly knew this was an absurdly and artificially low figure. Trying to assess the impact of labor, materials, and supervisory costs, together with the allocation of overhead and utility services as she had been taught to do, she came up with figures between $15 and $18 per transaction. In theory, interlibrary lending and borrowing were self-canceling processes, but Polly knew that it didn't work out that way in practice. There were net lenders and net borrowers.

Crossley was clearly a net lender, but why? Its collection was not any more extensive than that of any other good liberal arts college, but it was well organized, it had no broken runs for missing volumes, and it responded rapidly to external as well as internal patrons. That was the result of the philosophy Polly had instilled in her staff. The state university, by contrast, had a larger collection, but waiting six weeks for fulfillment was not unusual. And so, given the choice, most libraries turned to Crossley. Not just academic libraries, most of which were in even smaller colleges, but public, school, and occasional corporate libraries. By contrast, Crossley borrowed relatively little—in part because the collection had been carefully developed to start with, in part because the curriculum had not changed very much and Crossley had begun no new degree programs, and in part because in Crossley's liberal arts setting neither the students (there were no graduate students) nor the faculty did very much external research. The emphasis was on solid teaching, and that was something Crossley did very well.

As Polly looked at the statistics for recent months, she saw that during an average week Crossley had furnished 135 items on interlibrary loan to other institutions in the state, for which it had received the $5 support, while borrowing an average of 30. Most of the transactions were still coming through the mail on ALA interlibrary loan forms; while the Crossley Library had a FAX machine, many of the other participants did not.

Polly's calculations were simple. If interlibrary loans cost $15 per transaction, then Crossley had provided in each week $2,025 in services, or more than $100,000 per year. It received from the state less than $34,000. Even if forced to pay at the same rate for what it borrowed, that would only come to $22,500. In a free market system Crossley was losing over $40,000 a year on this process. So much for state subsidies! That kind of money would have paid for a desperately needed reference librarian, some expanded technology, or some combination of needs.

Polly, like just about any librarian, believed strongly in interlibrary cooperation, but this seemed more like taxation or confiscation. She could, of course, like the state university library, decrease the quality of response and increase the response time, discouraging requests through those methods. She knew that some other libraries did exactly that, if not deliberately then at least by not caring very much. She didn't have the stomach for that. It went counter to her whole philosophy of library service. Perhaps she needed to inform her college president of the implications of this process for Crossley. If the president knew, and agreed that it was nevertheless a worthwhile or at least unavoidable part of regional community relations, then she need have no further qualms. However, what if the president were horrified at this news and told her to cut way back, perhaps to a level of satisfying only as many requests as she herself transmitted? How could she then face her colleagues in professional meetings?

35

MY NIECE NEEDS A JOB

"Hello, Jim, this is Harry Eberstadt," the voice on the other end of the phone boomed. Library director James Bryant wouldn't have needed the identification to recognize the speaker. He found Eberstadt's voice both distinctive and irritating, but perhaps that was the kind of voice and mannerism useful in real estate development. Eberstadt was an appointed member of the public library board, and board members had the telephone number for direct access to Bryant's personal office without having to go through the switchboard.

"I don't want to take a lot of your time, Jimbo," Eberstadt continued. "I know you're very busy. At least you keep telling us how understaffed the library always is." Eberstadt laughed loudly at his own joke, which Bryant did not consider funny. "It just occurred to me that you didn't know that my niece, Amy Carlson, is studying to be a librarian in the master's program at the state university. Her mother just told my wife that Amy would be applying for one of your children's librarian jobs that you always complain are so hard to fill. Well, I can tell you Amy will be just great. She's smart, she's sweet, and she loves books and working with kids. I just thought I'd alert you, since she's lucky enough not to have the same last name as her uncle. I also want to assure you that she's nowhere near as obnoxious as I am." More laughter followed.

Bryant became immediately defensive. "You do understand, don't you, Harry, that we have to follow all sorts of official procedures to make sure we hire the best person? Tell your niece to contact the personnel department for the application materials, and personnel will take it from there. I really don't play any role at all in selecting beginning children's librarians."

"Sure, I understand." Eberstadt's voice was smooth and reassuring. "I just though you'd want to know. Take care now."

James Bryant hadn't wanted to know, and the telephone call annoyed him, as indeed Eberstadt's mannerisms frequently annoyed him. In reality, he had told Harry a slight untruth. It was correct that the application process began with the personnel department, but all finalists were interviewed by the director, and the director made the ultimate decision from among those considered acceptable by personnel and the immediate chain of supervision. He would be making the final decision about hiring any children's librarians. And even though there would probably be a shortage of qualified applicants, he already knew that he didn't want to hire Harry Eberstadt's niece. He also realized that this was unfair to Amy Carlson, about whom he knew nothing at all. But then, isn't it also unfair to have a stupid jerk for an uncle?

36

PUBLIC AND CORPORATE ETHICS

Connie had been librarian at the Metropolitan Development Corporation for six months. She had taken the job straight out of library school, and since her M.L.S. had immediately followed the completion of her bachelor's degree in economics, this was really her first regular job, with supervisory responsibilities in a dynamic business organization. She felt pleased at her accomplishment. After all, she was only two months past her twenty-third birthday!

Metropolitan was primarily involved in real estate planning, developing parcels of land for industrial and business construction, although occasionally the company also involved itself in condominiums and hotels. The scope of its operation was international, and Connie found it an exciting and dynamic place to work. The questions and problems channeled to her as librarian exceeded anything that had been dealt with in any of her school courses, but she had been well educated, she was bright and curious, and she had done well. She knew the corporate management only slightly, but she sensed that they were very satisfied with her.

Although Metropolitan was global in the scope of its activities, one of its local initiatives had generated a great deal of attention and controversy. The company had proposed razing six downtown city blocks that held generally crumbling row houses, tenements, bars, and cheap hotels, and replacing them with single- and multifamily dwellings for lower and middle income groups. This had been recommended as a desperately needed rejuvenation of a stagnant section of the inner city. Although concerns had been raised about the thousands of people who would be displaced in the process, it had been countered that many of these individuals would be relocated right back into their old neighborhoods, into a far better quality of life, after the renovations were done. No final decision by the city council had been made, but the mayor supported the plan and it was likely to be approved.

The library was located right next to the corporate administrative offices, and Connie thought it was a good location from which to cultivate contacts with the top executives. Although not yet well acquainted with the executives, Connie already knew the corporate secretarial staff quite well. Several of them were her contemporaries, and she shared occasional coffee breaks and lunches with them. There was another advantage. The library, like most special libraries, did a great deal of photocopying and had its own copying machine. However, on those occasions when her machine was in need of repair, Connie had no problem in using the corporate offices' copying equipment, which was actually better and faster. The courtesy, of course, applied both ways.

Today the library copier was in need of repair, and Connie took a stack of journals next door. That copier was not in use, and Amanda, who was on the phone, just waved her in. Connie always tried to finish her copying tasks there as quickly as possible, and if necessary do the collating back in the library. As she did this today, she found an extra piece of paper. It had probably been inadvertently left in the tray by the last person who used the machine. That could have been any of the four support staff people, or even executives, who often made their own copies.

This was a memorandum from Albert Lee, vice-president for planning, addressed to Edward R. Hayes, president and chief executive officer, under the subject Downtown Project. It said: "I've rechecked my calculations again, and I'm even more convinced that building low and medium income housing on the downtown tract is not going to be break-even, let alone profitable. Interest rates for home mortgages are high and probably going higher, and there is no certainty of the continuation of rent subsidies at either the federal or municipal level. We could get stuck with vacant lots, or with completed buildings without buyers. By contrast, my projections still show that if we could turn this property into an upscale shopping mall, with theatres, restaurants, and plenty of convenient parking, there are several major national department stores that could be interested in serving as anchors for it. Such an approach, in my judgment, is as close to a sure bet as anything can be. I realize, of course, that we can't spring this on the city administration at this time, because we would never get approval. I would therefore suggest that we proceed with stage one, approval to clear the site of existing buildings, and then examine our options when this is completed. If confronted by six blocks of empty downtown space, the city administration will almost have to go along with whatever we propose."

The memorandum was stamped *strictly confidential,* and as Connie read it she became very angry. She understood that property development was a high risk and creative enterprise, but she had not bargained for being part of what she considered simply fraud and misrepresentation. She thought that if she were to send copies of this memorandum anonymously to the local newspapers and TV stations, taking reasonable precautions, she would never be suspected. Only Amanda might remember that she had used the corporate office copier today, and lots of other people used it regularly. Without a log-in sheet nobody would even know the sequence in which copies had been made. After all, she didn't even work in that office. Why would anybody think of her? She was still idealistic enough to be tempted to expose this reprehensible behavior.

37

A CASE OF DE FACTO SELF-SEGREGATION

It was the Reverend Emanuel Washington who had first raised the point at the meeting of the board of trustees. Library director Elizabeth Moberley had just completed her report on the number of minority staff members and on the library's attempts to implement its affirmative action agenda. There had been some progress at the Empire City and County Public Library, but progress had been disappointingly slow. Nevertheless, Elizabeth felt no apprehension about presenting her report. The library board had been both supportive and encouraging, and even minority leaders such as the Reverend Washington were positively inclined and not at all accusative. It was a good board, Elizabeth thought, one that cared about the city and the library. Even when they might disagree, they did so with courtesy and fairness. There was no political posturing.

Elizabeth had just finished this section of her report, in which she noted both the statistics and the ongoing programs to support library employees, and particularly black and hispanic employees, as they pursued library degrees on a part-time basis with both financial and schedule flexibility support from the library. Progress was slow, but there *was* progress. It was at this point that Pastor Washington had spoken out. "I don't want in any way to minimize what you have done, Elizabeth," he said, "but do you realize that even when we have succeeded in increasing the representation of minority staff members we have not succeeded in increasing their visibility, that we have kept them in a sort of library ghetto? To my observation, black librarians work in the branches that serve the inner city and in the main library, which is also in the inner city. The suburban branches, which serve at least to some extent the whites who have fled the inner city, have almost exclusively white patrons and white staff members."

Elizabeth realized immediately that this was true, although there was certainly no library policy to establish any such pattern. It had just happened that way over time. She agreed with Emanuel Washington that this was morally wrong and counterproductive to the goal of establishing an integrated community, at least insofar as the library was concerned. The rest of the board members had also quickly and unanimously agreed, and instructed the library administration to take steps to assure a dispersal of personnel of all racial and ethnic backgrounds throughout the library system.

Elizabeth had expected some static from whites who were going to be assigned to inner city branches, based on the predictable arguments about safety and security, and this had indeed happened. She had not, however, expected similar objections and opposition from the minority staff members who now worked there. The reasons expressed varied, but they all seemed, at least on first hearing, very sincere. It turned out that the staffing patterns in branches and in the main library were far more a matter of design and planning—not by the library, but by the staff members themselves—than she had realized. Some individuals wanted, insofar as possible, to work within a short commuting distance of their homes, and they resented this complication that was being imposed for what they considered a capricious reason. Working mothers and single parents in particular expressed this concern. They liked working in a branch only several blocks from where their children were after school, and Elizabeth could see the point. However, she also found that many black and hispanic staff members specifically preferred to work in branches where they felt they could provide more direct assistance to members of their own groups and serve as effective role models for children in particular. When word of the impending mass transfers got out, parents, and particularly inner-city parents, chimed in with the same complaint. "Give us better library collections, more attractive buildings, longer library hours and better budgets, but leave us the staff we love and respect" was the underlying refrain.

Elizabeth began to realize that what had been so easily mandated might really prove to be counterproductive, and would in any case be difficult. Because there were more white than minority staff members she could probably more easily force some whites to transfer to the inner city, but should she really scatter what few minority staff she had into the suburban branches?

Conscious and deliberate segregation on the basis of race and color had been illegal since Brown *vs.* Board of Education and other similar cases, but judges had also ruled that de facto segregation, even when unplanned as such, had to be rectified. The Empire County Public School system had been involved in court-mandated busing for some time, although there was also a good deal of discussion about whether this was a good idea, compared to a greater emphasis on improving local schools. Exposure to different people was certainly a laudable and democratizing experience, but what should she do about these cases involving the public library that were really a matter of self-segregation?

38

PICK A BRANCH LIBRARY TO CLOSE

Along with other municipal agencies, the Brookton Public Library and its director, Barbara Hanover, had approached the mayoral elections with some apprehension. Officially silenced by their governmental status, the library employees nevertheless had their rooting interest. Brookton was an industrial community in what had been heavily industrialized New England. However, what had befallen Brookton was not atypical in the area. Industrial flight to the nonunion South and Mexico and overseas, combined with aging and obsolete plants and equipment, had increased unemployment in a population that had become increasingly black and hispanic as well as older. Middle-class whites and many businesses had fled to the suburbs and suburban malls as well as to other states. The cost of municipal services had grown rapidly, and the tax base with which to pay for these services had steadily eroded. Real estate taxes, the backbone for the support of much municipal service—including library service—were very high. Barbara knew, because she was among those who paid those taxes.

In the midst of this pessimism had suddenly appeared Oliver Crafton, a newcomer to local politics. Crafton had been president of Excelsior Electronics, a military contractor that had managed to maintain profitability, although it was not certain whether this was because of astute management or the sheer luck of global tensions. Crafton had retired at the age of 56 after selling his company to an international conglomerate. He was a millionaire and still vigorous, and whether he entered the political arena from conviction or because he was bored was open to speculation—and was indeed the subject of speculation. Perhaps a little of both, Barbara thought. She didn't like Crafton and what she considered his simplistic message, but she tried to be fair.

Crafton's appeal had certainly been simple if not merely simplistic. He argued that what Brookton needed was a government based on corporate decision models. Industry understood, as public servants did not, he continually emphasized, that priorities had to be established to decide what could and could not be done. The cow that had been milked for public funding was running dry, and indeed he adopted a picture of an emaciated cow as the campaign symbol for the movement that he and like-minded independents had established. Although he was probably thought of as a politically conservative independent, he had broken with both of the traditional parties. His theme was direct, and he repeated it over and over: Brookton needed to be run like a business, and priorities had to be established. He was just the man to do that, because he had spent his whole career saying no to people who didn't like to hear the word. Brookton needed a tough manager who would make tough decisions and who would say no to the municipal hangers-on who sought only to feather their own nests. Under his administration there would be austerity, but he promised to preserve all services that were really essential. Taxes had to come down if Brookton were to have any hope of stemming industrial exodus and reestablishing the community values of which they all felt proud.

That was his entire message. There were no details on how he was going to accomplish this. He parried all questions by saying that specific decisions would be made quickly once he had all the facts. Crafton's newly created Taxpayer's Party had contested not only for the mayor's office, but also for every vacant council seat. Municipal employees, as well as many citizen groups and of course the underprivileged, saw themselves as directly threatened by this rhetoric. Barbara guessed that in all probability not one single library employee had voted for the Crafton slate. But others obviously had, because the Taxpayer's Party had won, and won impressively all across the board. Crafton now controlled the city council. The local newspaper and the two TV stations, which had remained officially neutral during the campaign, now jumped on the bandwagon and expressed optimism for a leaner but better and brighter Brookton.

True to his word, Crafton did not delay implementation of his philosophy. He took office on January 1, and by January 15 he would have concluded meetings with the heads of every municipal agency. As these municipal leaders, her friends and colleagues, emerged from their sessions battered and bleeding and reported back to Barbara what had transpired, she had only the worst to fear. She was to be Crafton's last scheduled appointment, at 2:00 on January 15.

On balance, the meeting did not go nearly as badly as she had imagined, and yet there was a huge problem. Crafton was relaxed and affable. He told Barbara that he had saved the library for last because he didn't really think it posed major problems. He supported libraries, and he thought that this library was rather well run and far more effective in giving the city its money's worth than some of the agencies he was planning to clobber. Having a strong library would also be important for the city image he wanted to create, and he would be talking to her at a later date about strengthening the business information service, which would be a part of his campaign to attract new industry.

Although he didn't consider the library a major problem, he felt that it must participate in the prioritizing and cost-cutting activities, so that others would not complain of favoritism. "I'll tell you how we'll do this, Barbara," he had stated with authority and conviction. "I want you to run cost-effectiveness studies comparing all your branches. The easiest way to have the taxpayers understand is to divide the total cost of running the branch, including everything—labor, materials, utilities—by the circulation, which you always prominently report in your annual reports anyway. That will give us a ranking of your branches in order of importance and efficiency, and we'll close the bottom branch as a token gesture. With some luck, one is all we'll have to close, but I can't promise right now. I don't need to tell you that you're getting off a lot easier than all of the other department heads. When the right time comes, we'll even get you some more money for computerization and that business information program I talked about and really jazz things up."

As Barbara left, she had to agree that she had gotten off much more easily than she had expected, but she saw the huge problem she faced. She could and would look at the cost-effectiveness data Crafton had ordered. That was easy enough, but she already knew what that would show, and she also knew that there were other factors in evaluating library services besides dollars and cents. Should she have raised this point in this initial meeting? Would it have done any good, or might it have soured the start of the relationship? In any case, she hadn't done it.

Barbara knew that playing by Crafton's rules, the branch to close was the Martin Luther King branch. It had been opened only two years ago, to strengthen library services and bring literacy programs to the most disadvantaged area of the city. There had been progress in increasing the use of this new branch, but real progress took time. Many of these people had little history of using libraries. The King branch was an investment in a better future for the citizens of Brookton. It could not be expected to turn an immediate "profit."

If Barbara decided to fight this closing, to whom would she turn for help? Crafton had not built his political victory on the votes of inner-city ghetto residents. Those wards had all opposed him, and he knew it. The library board had always been supportive of but never particularly active in politics. The nine members served three-year rotating terms. Crafton would be appointing three members almost immediately, and she didn't know what he had in mind. In another year he could control the majority of the board, and he had a four-year term as mayor. However, even in the present year Barbara doubted that the holdovers would have any stomach for tackling Crafton head-on. They included two people from the business community, a doctor, two individuals who could be classified most simply as parents and homemakers, and one teacher who was black and had been very instrumental in the process of developing the MLK branch. This board member would naturally be devastated by any plans to close that branch after two years of high hopes and expectations.

39
REJECTION OF A TAX APPEAL

Margaret Rutkowski did not enter her comfortable director's office at the Fillmore Public Library with her usual enthusiasm this morning. She knew why, of course, but she was nevertheless conscious of the fact that her depression was unusual. It really hadn't been a bad four years. She had come to Fillmore from an assistant director's position in a large city, and adjusting to the ways of living and decision-making of this midwestern community had taken a little time. Fillmore was a pleasant place to live, with quiet tree-lined residential neighborhoods, and a church-run college that didn't provide a great deal of cultural activity but did offer an occasional lecture and even a recital from time to time. There were sporting events, and although you knew that probably none of these athletes was ever going to make it to the pros, the competition could be just as exciting. Fillmore offered a slower life-style, but Margaret, as a single mother with a teen-age daughter, had found it a good place to live.

Nor was Fillmore really a sleepy little town. There was a good deal of civic pride, and Margaret had been able to parlay that into some genuine improvements for the library. The library hadn't really been bad before she came; the better word was probably unimaginative. She had been able to attract some strong new subordinates as vacancies occurred, and she had been fortunate in the fact that her arrival had coincided with a number of retirements and relocations of individuals whose departure she did not mourn. The staff was now definitely stronger, and shared her enthusiasm. They had been able to implement a business information service that pleased the chamber of commerce; they worked with local civic groups to develop an adult literacy program, added materials services to shut-ins, implemented the beginning of on-line and CD-ROM services, and innovated new programming in the children's department that was everybody's pride and joy. She had good rapport with and strong editorial support from the local newspaper, which was really pretty dull most of the time but was important to have on your side. The Friends of the Library group, which she had reactivated, was not really a political force, but it was helpful in raising public consciousness; and its fund-raising efforts paid for some of the peripheral services and equipment, particularly in the children's and young adults' room.

It had been clear enough to her right from the beginning that there was really only one source of local political power, and that was Mayor Dominic Dallessandro. He had been mayor for fourteen years, and his style was one that Margaret would have to categorize as benevolent despotism. There was no hint of dishonesty or corruption in his administration. Dom was genuinely committed to the good of Fillmore—Margaret was convinced of that—but he also had clear ideas of what that good ought to be. One did not cross Mayor Dallessandro except at great peril, and probably to no useful result. To suggest that the mayor controlled everything was an exaggeration, but it was probably more true that he controlled whatever in Fillmore he cared enough to control. His style was that of the velvet fist. Everybody understood his power, and probably also accepted the premise of his concern for the well-being of the community. In her four years she could not recall any major political conflicts. Local officials ran as nonpartisans; and although Dallessandro was nominally a Democrat, at least to the extent of serving as Democratic convention delegate, he was really above party labels. Since he had evidenced no political ambitions beyond his present office, the state politicians did not pick fights with him, not even the Republicans. Dallessandro controlled the library board, but Margaret, who had at first been concerned about this, soon realized that it wasn't really a problem. All of the board members were appointed for overlapping terms, and the mayor either appointed them directly or strongly influenced the people who did the appointing. However, the members were good people, committed to a strong community of Fillmore and to a strong library as part of that strategy. Both the board and the mayor supported her initiatives, because she had learned to present them not in the narrow context of the library, but in the larger sense of a better Fillmore. Her library school teacher had been right: Recognizing that the library was not an end in itself but rather a means to an end, and then publicizing that end, worked.

One thing that Mayor Dallessandro did not control was the tax base and tax allocation that supported the library. The library received a fixed percentage of collected taxes, and that percentage could, by action of the state legislature, be changed only by the approval of the board of tax appeal, a body the mayor did not appoint or have a hold upon. Margaret was sure that the mayor had influence in just about any area in which he chose to use it, but she recognized that he played his cards carefully and applied pressure only when he felt it was really important enough.

The library's innovative programs then ran into the brick wall of funding limitations imposed without regard to needs and justifications, and that was frustrating. It could have been worse. At least Fillmore was still growing, unlike other communities in the state, and the tax base was rising even if slowly. However, it was rising far *too* slowly to permit funding of the new services that Margaret wanted, the community wanted, and the board wanted as soon as it had reassured itself that the mayor was also in agreement.

She had discussed the dilemma frequently with the board, and on two occasions in a meeting that the mayor attended, and it was agreed that a tax appeal to request a larger funding share would have to be filed and argued. Mayor Dallessandro seemed certain that success would be achieved, but he urged that the new programs be started even in the expectation of the new funding. That way, he noted quite confidently, the state board of tax appeal would be dealing with a real issue and with real services that people really wanted. You had to have a need before you could justify assistance. Too many people cried wolf before they were hurt. That didn't work, but this strategy was bound to. The mayor seemed so certain of this that he had persuaded not only the library board, but also Margaret herself. So they had started programs for which they really didn't have the money, borrowing future funds against the success of the tax appeal. The community had responded with enthusiasm to new initiatives that encompassed everybody, from children to retirees, from adult learners to the business community.

And then it was time to present the case for the tax appeal. True to his word, the mayor had delegated his fiscal advisor to help put together the documentation, because in this kind of endeavor Margaret was in a little over her head. The newspaper had contributed supportive articles and editorials, and the Friends of the Library, well intentioned but not really well focused for such a task, had done what they could.

The final document, Margaret felt, looked good. It was a solid and professional effort, and it had unanimous support—at least on the surface.

Margaret was not naive. She understood that these cases were not necessarily decided on their merits. There needed to be some behind-the-scenes lobbying and the application of pressure. Here she had to depend on Mayor Dallessandro, and she couldn't really know how hard her champion had fought for her behind the scenes. She could only hope. There really was no point in conjecture. The mayor obviously had his own priorities. How high the library ranked she could not tell.

But the board of tax appeal had rejected the Fillmore Library Board's request. Everyone was sympathetic, pointing out that tax appeals rarely make it though the process in an election year, and that the governor had just been reelected on a pledge of belt-tightening and hold-the-line expenditures. Margaret suddenly found herself surrounded by 20/20 hindsight that made perfectly plausible what up to now nobody had even suggested was possible. There were even reassurances that the appeal would have a much better chance next year, or at worst in two years. She just had to be patient.

But Margaret knew, and certainly everyone should have known although suddenly nobody seemed to notice, that the problem was much more serious than just a rejection of new funding. The library was spending money it simply did not have, and at this rate would run out of money two months before the end of the fiscal year. Drastic cuts had to be implemented immediately, and much as this hurt, some of the new initiatives just started would have to be shelved just as quickly. Margaret recognized that it was her job to present the options to the board for their approval, just as the board would be looking to City Hall for its signals. She realized that she needed to involve the city's budget planning department as well as the board in this exercise. Undoubtedly the mayor as well would want to participate in deciding priorities.

Margaret got out a large pad of paper and began a list headed "Things That Could Be Deferred with Implications of Deferral" when her secretary buzzed her on the intercom. The call was from Sally Rogers, Mayor Dallessandro's longtime administrative assistant. When Sally spoke it was with the voice of the mayor, and the opinions she expressed had been specifically formulated by him. Sally came straight to the point. She was calling at the instruction of Mayor Dallessandro. The mayor regretted not being able to talk to Margaret about this directly, but he had just left for a three-day reunion of his old Korean War army unit. Margaret knew, as did everyone in Fillmore, of Dallessandro's impressive military record. He had been awarded the Distinguished Service Cross, as well as two Purple Hearts, and he had been involved in some heavy fighting. Margaret was certain that the war record was genuine, but it certainly hadn't hurt him politically.

Sally went on to convey the mayor's deep disappointment at the actions of the board of tax appeal, but he wanted to stress that by no means did he consider such actions to be final. It might be possible to submit a new and strengthened appeal next year, although it might be more prudent to wait two years. These were issues he would be happy to discuss with Margaret and the members of the board after his return and a suitable period for thinking about alternatives. One month from now might be a good time to target the meeting. The mayor urged her to remain positive and cheerful. Things would work out just fine.

However, there was one piece of urgent business, and that was really the main purpose of the phone call. The denial of the tax appeal had received prominent mention on the evening television newscast, and a front-page story would be appearing in this afternoon's paper. (Margaret could not help but be impressed that the mayor already knew that.) Dallessandro had already received a number of concerned telephone calls from individuals worried about the library's programs, and in particular the new initiatives. These individuals, and others, needed immediate reassurance. He wanted Margaret to call a news conference for this morning to issue a statement that despite the denial of the tax appeal, services to the citizens of Fillmore from their fine public library would not be affected, and current programs would continue with their usual quality and vigor.

Margaret knew there was no point in arguing with Sally Rogers. Sally only conveyed messages. She did not make policy, and she could not change this instruction even if she wanted to. Margaret did have the presence of mind to ask Sally if the mayor could be reached by phone. Sally said this would be quite impossible. Today the mayor would be en route in his car; starting tonight he would be at the reunion, which would last three days and which would be held in a simulated bivouac area in the middle of a national park. Dallessandro might call in for messages during this period, but she wasn't sure. There did not appear to be anything of great urgency on his agenda.

40

THE GIFT OF A WHITE ELEPHANT

University president Maxwell Shoemaker was being patient, he thought, but it seemed to library director Joanna Miller that he was also being condescending. Shoemaker explained one more time that the proffered gift of the Hazeltyne collection of the literature of the American West might or might not contain a great many gold nuggets, but that the collection was only the forerunner of other and much larger donations, which would involve money and not just books. The university could not afford to antagonize John D. Hazeltyne, because there were other institutions of higher education that would happily take his money. Hazeltyne was undoubtedly an eccentric. It was likely that his collecting habits were not based on sound scholarly principles. However, Hazeltyne was a very rich eccentric, eighty years old and a confirmed bachelor without obvious heirs. There were not only suggestions of future donations in the next few years to finance a student center and dormitory to be named after him, but Hazeltyne had also been carefully cultivated by the university to arouse his interest in establishing a major endowment after his death. This could amount to $50 million or even more. The acceptance of Hazeltyne's "research" collection (and Shoemaker would agree with Miller in the privacy of her office that scholars might consider it largely junk from a historical standpoint) was apparently Hazeltyne's test of the university's sincerity.

Miller responded again that she understood all that. She was prepared to take the entire collection, send Hazeltyne an elaborate letter of thanks, and turn the materials over to the collection development staff and the history specialist in the University library, using history faculty for advice, evaluation, and the process of weeding out some material. But keeping the collection as a separately housed entity in a unique room would be a waste of valuable library space. Furthermore, it would make them an academic laughing stock.

"I doubt that," Shoemaker replied. "There are plenty of universities and their librarians who would accept this offer, and if we get the rest of the Hazeltyne money nobody will be laughing. Some of that money will go to the library. Don't forget that, Joanna. I agree that putting this into a separate room doesn't make much sense, but that is what he insists on. Fortunately, with the new building you just moved into last year you have the space to accommodate the collection as an entity, at least for the present. After that, we'll see. I don't expect full cataloging for this stuff and I doubt that Hazeltyne will think of asking for it. He just wants to see it prominently displayed in a room with nice furniture. I'll give you the money for that, and insofar as this adds other costs to the library let me know what they are and I'm sure we can work something out. Look, I really don't want to discuss this any more. I want you to write Hazeltyne a letter telling him how thrilled you are to be getting his collection of research materials, and that you're happy to agree to his conditions. I've already told him that for the university, but having it come from you will impress him."

41

THE SHOEMAKER'S CHILDREN ARE THE LAST TO GET SHOES

The Magnum Chemical Company Information Center had reported to the vice-president for corporate planning for over ten years. It was, for the information center and its manager, Marjorie Bartkowski, a good relationship. The vice-president was not only a solid supporter of information services, he was also a powerful and experienced figure in the corporate political arena. Although Magnum was undergoing some difficult times and undertaking personnel reductions through attrition, the impact on the information center was somewhat ameliorated by a heavy emphasis on automation; this reduced its reliance on clerical staff, and also permitted the implementation of a number of in-house operational systems that did not require much internal staff support from Marjorie and ran on corporate computer hardware. Information files were purchased and downloaded for central processing, and internal files were created and merged with them for ease of information access. Periodical checking and missing issue claims, bindery procedures, circulation, overdue notices, selective dissemination of information, and bibliographic compilations all were in place and solidly supported by a strong and helpful systems organization that included both systems software and hardware operations. As might be imagined, systems work in support of the information center was continuous and involved new projects, systems changes, and maintenance.

When the vice-president for planning retired, Marjorie truly felt the loss of a good friend. His replacement, who came from the marketing organization, was not a heavy information center user, and expressed reluctance to have the information center report to him. The corporate management decision to have the information center report to Charley Horvath, director of technology and computer systems, did not displease Marjorie. She had worked well with Charley and his people in the past. They were excellent professionals who had met and even exceeded her expectations of support services. It seemed to her that in reporting to Charley's organization, the information center would be in an even better position to take advantage of opportunities to provide enhanced information services through computer access, particularly since a corporate-wide hiring freeze had been in effect for all but critical replacements for the last year.

However, she noticed almost immediately a drop-off in service support from the other members of the organization of which she was now a part. Schedules started to slip, key systems personnel were pulled off information center projects and replaced, after delays, by junior people who then had to learn the tasks to be performed. She mentioned her concerns to Charley

Horvath, who suggested they have lunch so they could talk. He was direct and frank, but not very helpful. He regretted the dilution in support services, but he was aware of them and had even to some extent dictated them. The manpower ceilings throughout Magnum had been very difficult to manage in his organization because demand for support services continued to increase from all areas of the corporation. It was essential that he continue to maintain a strong image for his organization; also, in that approach lay the only eventual hope for exemption from the hiring freeze. When that happened Marjorie would get better service. It was also obviously crucial, at this critical time, that he deal most directly with the requirements that had the highest political priority and the greatest demonstrated impact on profits. Unfortunately, that did not include the information center. Moreover, by giving other projects greater priority he avoided possible charges of favoritism. He expected her to be a good soldier and to cooperate until things got better.

Marjorie now realized that much of the reason for her strong past support came not because of Charley Horvath but from the power exerted by the vice-president for planning, an individual unfortunately now living in southern Florida and not available to help her.

42

THE SCHOOL LIBRARY AS DETENTION CENTER

Melissa Moncrief was both confident and a little nervous. Although she was only 24 and this was her first "real" professional job, she felt well prepared. She had wanted to be a school librarian for as long as she could remember, and had obtained her M.L.S. making sure that she met all of the school certification requirements. The interviews at the Harrison County School system had gone well, and when offered the job as school media specialist at the Macklin Middle School, she had accepted without hesitation. Harrison County was in her home state about 150 miles from where she had grown up. She liked and understood these people, and she was particularly attracted by the opportunity to work with middle school–age pupils, because she thought they were at a crucial age in the formation of attitudes toward libraries and learning.

She had started just shortly before the start of the school year in early September, and it was now the middle of October. She was still feeling her way around, and she now knew that there were problems in the attitudes of some of the pupils and teachers, and of course money problems. However, most people had been both friendly and supportive, and principal Adelaide Hockenberry had told Melissa to come to her any time she had a concern or a problem. Melissa was determined to make the school's media and learning center both a useful and friendly place. She had begun to establish a good rapport with some of the students, although she didn't yet know many of them. She had sent a memorandum to all the teachers explaining her desire to be helpful in integrating the library into their curriculum programs and asking them to talk to her about ways in which they could work together. A couple of them already had, and she was sure there would be more.

The note from teacher Andrea McGinnis required further clarification, and today's teachers meeting would give her the opportunity to follow up with a person she might have met but didn't really remember. It was a large school. The note simply informed "the librarian" that student James Moran was being assigned to stay in the library for the fifth period for the entire next week, and asked the librarian to monitor his attendance and report any absence. The message needed clarification, and after the meeting Melissa asked one of the teachers she did know to point out Andrea McGinnis.

"I received your note, and I'll be glad to supervise James in the library next week. What's the project he's supposed to be working on?"

"I don't care what he works on," McGinnis replied. "He is being sent to the library as punishment for repeatedly disturbing the class, and with the approval of Dr. Hockenberry. What we're doing is depriving him of his outside recreation period for one week. Perhaps that might impress him enough to behave himself for a while."

Melissa was disturbed at this news. She pointed out that it was her aim to have the media center seen as a friendly and useful place. She didn't want it perceived as some sort of jail or punishment, because that would completely contradict the image she was trying to create.

"You're new around here," McGinnis responded. "There are some things you need to learn. I think your ideas for the library are great, and I wish you luck with them. However, we do have disciplinary problems, and when you have disciplinary problems you can't teach the rest of the class. We've used assignment to the library as a punishment for quite a while, and I'm surprised that this is the first case this semester. It doesn't work perfectly, but it works better than anything else we've been able to think of. We don't have a detention room and we wouldn't have the staff to monitor one if we did. Hockenberry doesn't want us to use her office. The library is open and staffed, and it's the only place in which there isn't anything organized going on. If Jimmy finds something useful to do I certainly won't mind, but knowing him I would be surprised. However, the point of all this is to make him do something he would rather not do. Otherwise it wouldn't be very effective punishment, would it? Most of these kids don't like having to go to the library, and as long as that's true we have at least one tactic we can use. We have few enough."

43

THE FRILLS OF PUBLIC LIBRARY ON-LINE SEARCHING

Sybil Thornbush felt as though she were treading water. The board members seemed patient with her arguments, almost to the point of being patronizing, as if she were a child. She felt reasonably confident that if she could ever get past Walter Cunningham, she might have a case with the rest of the public library board. But Walter, with the cold and calculating logic of the successful banker he was, would not be moved, and the others followed his lead.

"Let me recap once again," Walter said in his dry and metronomic voice. Sybil knew that Walter was really a strong library supporter, it was just that he saw everything so logically, and logic to him meant dollars and cents. "You have asked us to start a program of on-line searching for the citizens of this community, and we have agreed that this would indeed be useful. We have approved funding of the computer hardware from our capital funds, and will absorb the salary costs of the reference librarians who will be performing the searches. The line costs, however, are linear, and you can't tell us what they will be. It depends on the data base, and on how successful the service becomes. In other words, the more successful we are the more trouble we get into. I consider it both fair and reasonable to expect the user for whom the search is being undertaken to reimburse the library for what the owner of the data base charges us—nothing more and nothing less. The budget for this library, I need not remind you, is fixed by the tax rate and the tax base. You are trying to sell us a pig in a poke, and I for one won't buy it. Neither, I suspect, will the others here."

Sybil knew this was certainly true, but she would try one more time. "The American Library Association has voted a number of times, and so has this state's library association, that all library services must be free. What you are proposing runs in complete contradiction to everything this profession stands for."

Walter sighed. "First of all, let me remind you that talk here, as everywhere, is cheap. The American Library Association can vote what it likes, but it does not fund this library, and it takes no responsibility for what happens here. Second, it could certainly be argued that on-line searching is not a basic right covered even under these interpretations. We still provide free service to everyone, we just restrict what we *can* provide with what we can house and predict within our budget. All we are doing is recovering extraordinary expenses. You charge for the use of the copier, and for interlibrary loan fees, don't you? How is this different?"

Sybil had heard this before, and so she tried another tack. "Suppose we *do* charge for the service and waive the fee for those unable to pay. You know who they are—mostly students, the elderly, the poor."

Walter's voice took on a tinge of sarcasm. "And how would you make the determination of who could pay? I'm a banker and half the time I can't tell. My kids have friends who can afford tickets to rock concerts I don't think I could afford. You'd be opening up a can of worms that would ultimately get this library into a mess of trouble. We either charge everybody or we charge nobody. And much as we would like to do that, we can't afford to charge nobody." Walter's voice took on the tone of finality that Sybil had come to recognize very well. "Look, this is your proposal, not ours. If you find the terms under which we are willing to approve on-line searching unacceptable to you, or to your interpretation of what the American Library Association and the state library association would have you do, then let's forget the whole thing. I assume that nobody has yet suggested that *every* library has to offer on-line searching whether it has the money or not."

44
A FIRING WITHOUT RECOURSE

When Virginia Maloney learned that Sandra Mancuso had been suddenly fired by the board of the Bellfort Public Library after twelve years of devoted service and without notice or warning, she was shocked but not really surprised. Bellfort had a reputation as a red-neck community in the rural area of the state, and Veronica's attempts to broaden library services to all the citizens of the community had not always been appreciated by groups of people who did not use libraries, did not much care what libraries did as long as they were cheap, and were suspicious of the role of librarians in poisoning the minds of children by exposing them to "dirty" books. In the last election, this point of view had seized majority control of the library board. Sandra, who was an old friend, had confided to Virginia that she did not look forward to the future and expected difficulties. Perhaps she should look for another job, but she and her husband were longtime residents of Bellfort and he could not simply relocate from his air conditioning and heating sales and service business. And now Sandra had been fired, on a casual motion made at what had appeared to be a routine meeting. The new majority had obviously planned this in advance. No reasons were given, and Sandra's supporters on the Board were as uniformed as she.

Because they were old friends, Virginia called to offer her support and comfort, and asked if she could come by to take Sandra to lunch. Friends need friends at times like this. However, Virginia had another reason. She was past president and still an executive board member of the state library association, and she wanted to know what the association might do to help, or at least to ward off a recurrence somewhere else.

Sandra's explanation at lunch added very little information. The new board members were obviously determined to get rid of her and to replace her with someone they could control. They had only awaited their first opportunity. Under new business at the board meeting a new member had simply proposed that the employment of the librarian be terminated. The motion had been seconded, and after some stunned protests by obviously unprepared minority members, the question had been put to a vote and passed. The votes had been there all along.

Had Sandra consulted an attorney? Yes, she had, but the news was not good. Library directors, unlike lower-level employees who did have rights of appeal, served specifically "at the pleasure of the board." That was not unusual in this state. Indeed, the same rule had applied to other municipal employees until, about fifteen years ago and in response to a particularly ugly incident, the state legislature had specifically exempted police and fire chiefs and school superintendents from the "pleasure of the employer" rule. Library directors were not included in the legislation. Naturally, they were free to negotiate with their employers any specific contractual language that would provide terms of employment and termination notice. In the absence of such specific agreements, and the attorney knew of no library in the state in which they existed, there was nothing. Firing her may have been a despicable thing to do, but she had no legal recourse.

Virginia was outraged, and she promised Sandra that even if nothing could be done to help her, some good would at least come out of this. As she drove home after their two-hour lunch, several strategies occurred to her. The state library association could take a position of censure against the Bellfort board. Properly publicized, it might stir the more responsible and fair-minded people in the community into doing something. The library association could begin a campaign to get the state legislature to include library directors in the protection already granted to others. Virginia suspected that the primary reason that librarians had not been included was not because anyone was opposed, but because nobody had thought of it. Finally, the state library association could begin a program of alerting public library directors to the risks they were under and urge them to insist on protective language in their employment agreements. It might even be possible to come up with some sort of standard clause that would be fair enough to fit into all situations.

She immediately called the executive director of the state library association, a paid employee and very knowledgeable about how to get things done in the state capital, to discuss these options. The staff member, who knew Sandra Mancuso, was equally distraught, or at least so she said. However, she felt that none of these tactics was an appropriate course of action for the state library association. Perhaps eight years ago they might have been, but not now. She reminded Virginia that at that time the state library association had merged with the library trustees association. The action had been taken as an economy measure, and because librarians and trustees invariably agreed on the need to urge the state legislature and the governor to support additional funding for public libraries in the state. However, this issue was different. The trustees on the board might agree that the actions in Bellfort were despicable, but they would not agree to any sort of sweeping denunciation of fellow trustees, and they would most specifically oppose any campaign that would reduce their own powers, though they planned to use them more fairly and reasonably. Bringing this issue to the joint board at the next meeting could well polarize it and cause irreparable damage to other initiatives. The executive director urged very strongly that while individual letters could certainly be written by friends, the issue should not be brought up at the board meeting.

Virginia Maloney realized for the first time that while librarians and trustees might indeed be bonded in their support of public libraries, they still represented the classic dichotomy of employee and employer and might have different views of what "support for public libraries" entailed. Virginia wondered what to do next.

45

ONE GOOD TURN MAY EVENTUALLY EARN ANOTHER

"Oh, there's one more little thing," Wayne Johnson said casually. Nancy Marlin stiffened in her seat. She had been through this process with Wayne before. He almost inevitably saved the most unpleasant news for last in their meetings, and then introduced it as though it were trivial. Nancy was librarian at Hermes Insurance Company; Wayne was the manager of administrative services and her supervisor. She had been at Hermes about five years, but Wayne had been her supervisor for only the last six months.

He was an individual almost totally devoid of spark and initiative. He had been at Hermes for over twenty-five years, and Nancy suspected that they didn't really know what to do with him. He had been given this post and several service units to supervise for no reason she could fathom. She was on good, and casual, terms with Dr. Rossman, the director of research, a heavy and appreciative library user. However, Dr. Rossman was not in her chain of command, which ultimately led to the vice-president of administration and finance, and Nancy thought she had better not raise the question with any of the library users, who were usually in research, the legal department, or actuarial services. Up to now Wayne had not caused her any problems. He expressed no particular interest in the library or in any subordinate units and caused her no difficulties so far. Still, Nancy wondered what kind of advocate he would be. The library had a number of pressing needs, including an upgrading of computer support, the addition of one more clerk, and—most of all—more space.

"I had lunch yesterday with Harvey Martin of Corporate Records. They've got about five filing cabinets of old legal documents that there has never been any use for, but apparently the attorneys feel we must keep them in the original form and not microfilm. Harvey has no room for them, and Archives, for some reason, won't take them. They don't require any work, they just need storing."

Nancy tried hard not to let an edge creep into her voice. "Wayne, I know all about those files. Harvey has been trying to peddle them to me for the last two years. First of all, we don't have the room, as you well know. We've had to microfilm a fair number of internal documents that would be more easily used in full size, just to conserve space. In addition to that, I resent anybody's trying to dump their odds and ends on us. This is a professional library, not a storeroom. Harvey Martin knows perfectly well I won't take them, and he knows why."

If Wayne Johnson was embarrassed he certainly didn't show it. He gave a little laugh. "Gee, Nancy, don't get all steamed up about it. I didn't realize you had already talked to Harvey about this. That old buzzard just hoodwinked me into thinking you'd even be glad to have the records. He made a big point of telling me we were getting practically new filing cabinets. If Legal ever let us dispose of the records, the filing cabinets are ours, and we can use them." Johnson waited for some sort of jolly rejoinder from Nancy, but there was none, and so he just went on in the same tone. "As I said, I'm sorry I didn't check with you, but it never occurred to me that you might object. What's done is done. I told old Harve that you'd take the files, so I guess you're stuck with them. Harvey owes us a favor now, and I'm sure this will all come out okay in the long run."

46

FIGURE OUT A WAY TO DO MORE

Assistant director for technical services Elizabeth Pasternak would have been angry if library director Doralynn Smiley hadn't been apologetic about the whole thing. Come to think of it, that seemed to be Doralynn's style. Always pleasant and congenial, she nevertheless did not come across, at least to Elizabeth, as a very effective representative of the library in its dealings either with the faculty or with university administration. And yet whenever something like this came up, Doralynn became apologetic to the point of being obsequious. It didn't really help, but it tended to defuse the resentment that had built up. Elizabeth, who had now seen this from Doralynn over the period of four years that the two women had worked together, couldn't help wondering whether the whole thing was a strategy.

The news was certainly bad. President Thomas Hoagland, with his eyes firmly set on an Ivy League appointment, had made quite a career of capturing for the university commitments of support, some of which fit better than others. Whenever a donation appeared to be more trouble than it was worth, Hoagland confided knowingly that one had to take this emotional gift in order to get the real money. Perhaps that would seem to be sound strategy, except that Elizabeth had never seen round two of the process.

Most of these adventures on the part of President Hoagland did not affect the library, but this one did, and it directly affected Elizabeth and her staff of overworked and much-maligned catalogers. As Doralynn had explained it, Hoagland had told her this morning that he had accepted the private collection of James Russell Lawrence, a very wealthy alumnus. Lawrence had gathered materials on the old American West. The collection was large, but nobody seemed to know whether it was very good. The fact that the old American West was not a research area for this university did not seem to bother Hoagland, but to Elizabeth it meant that in all probability perhaps half the materials being donated by Lawrence would be new to the library collection. They might be in the OCLC data base and not require original cataloging, but it would still be a lot of work. It was hard to estimate without having the specific titles, but the equivalent of a full three months of work for the entire cataloging department was not an unreasonable assumption.

That wasn't the worst part. As Doralynn related the information about the meeting, Hoagland had grandly promised Lawrence that all of this material would be cataloged and available for use within a year. It would not require separate housing as a collection (Hoagland even took credit for that "clever" bit of negotiating), but each item would carry a book plate.

That was the sum total of the message Doralynn had conveyed. There was no additional money for extra staff or even overtime. "I know it's going to be a problem, but do the best you can," Doralynn had said. "I have confidence in you."

Elizabeth understood her problems with the ineffectiveness of Doralynn and the perhaps resulting problems of President Hoagland running amok, at least as they affected the library, but she didn't have any idea about how to solve them. She didn't want to leave for another library. She liked the community, she owned her home outright, and she planned to retire here in another ten years. Nor did Elizabeth know what to do about this new problem of an additional workload of perhaps three months duration. Simply stretching out the normal backlog by an equivalent period of time seemed unthinkable. The backlog was already two years for material without priority status, and some faculty were complaining bitterly about that—with good reason, she thought.

47

PROGRAMMED FOR FAILURE?

As Khalid Morgan sat in his apartment and reviewed the events of the afternoon, his initial euphoria slowly turned to doubt. Khalid had joined the Parkfield Public Library immediately upon graduation from library school five years ago. An active student with some leadership qualities, a gift for self-expression, and a social conscience, Khalid had been a campus leader as president of the Black Student Union during his undergraduate career. That had sometimes led to activities that could interfere with the pursuit of a high grade-point average. Nevertheless, he was a hardworking if not intuitively brilliant student, and his B average had been good enough to get him into the library school of his choice. He could have gone to the university law school (many of his friends were surprised at his choice) but Khalid Morgan had long wanted to be a librarian. His mother and aunt were both librarians, and a love for books and reading and, most of all, for helping others had been ingrained in him since he was a small child.

Khalid had eschewed campus political activity while at library school. In part this was because library-science students were somewhat separated from the rest of the student body and in part because no significant issues demanding his involvement had arisen. Primarily it was because he felt he needed to devote his energies to his studies if he were to succeed at the level he had targeted for himself, which was at least a B+ average. This he had accomplished, and when Parkfield offered him the post of junior reference librarian he had accepted. He suspected that affirmative action criteria made him a particularly attractive candidate, but he had no qualms about accepting because he felt that he would be a strong reference librarian.

And he was sure he had been. Shortly after taking the job he had married his childhood sweetheart, and they now had a lively two-year-old girl. He enjoyed his work as a reference librarian, and two years ago he had been promoted with the removal of the term *junior* from his title. Most of all, he enjoyed working with people. It had occurred to him on more than one occasion that if the opportunity to manage were to arise he would seize it.

He had been thrust into the protest by the library's maintenance workers, almost all black or hispanic, almost by accident. There was no doubt that they were underpaid and exploited, and that their opportunities for growth and promotion were nonexistent. When they filed their salary grievance against the city and the library with the city's affirmative action office, they had turned to Khalid to help them in the preparation of their case and to ask him to speak on their behalf to the media. The case had received a good deal of publicity in the press and on television, and Khalid had appeared both on screen and in print. He recognized that this activity might not enhance his reputation with the library administration, particularly after the maintenance workers won their grievance complaint, but he could not have turned his back on their plea for help. He had discussed the issue with his wife, Juanita, and she had urged him to follow his conscience. He smiled at the thought that Juanita had always understood his needs and supported him.

All this had happened a year ago. Since that time there had been no mention of this issue in the library reference department or in his infrequent contacts with library administration. There was certainly nothing he could pinpoint to suggest any resentment, but he was smart enough to realize that if they felt any they would make sure not to show it. With the grievance now resolved, he had few contacts with the Parkfield Public Library maintenance workers—certainly not because Khalid was a snob, but simply because he shared few social interests with them. Khalid and his wife circulated in a group of young professionals like themselves, largely but not exclusively black. He was an active member of both the NAACP and the Urban League but had not taken positions of leadership and visibility. He might at some point, but he was still young and a newcomer to the community.

When personnel director Alex Horowitz called him into the office this morning and offered him the post of head of the Morton Avenue branch, Khalid had been thrilled. It was the management opportunity he had long sought, and it represented both a promotion and a substantial salary increase. Alex had been cordial, as he usually was when he had good news to import. Khalid remembered him as less cordial during the grievance dispute, but nothing was said about that this morning. Khalid, as a matter of routine, had asked for a day to think about the offer and to discuss it with his wife, but in his heart he knew he wanted the job, and that Juanita would pose no objections. Horowitz had agreed to the delay, and it had been decided that Khalid would stop by to give him his answer tomorrow.

Now, with their daughter fast asleep and his wife attending a class, Khalid was beginning to have second thoughts. The Morton Avenue branch, he knew, had been a troubled branch almost from the beginning. It was located in a neighborhood undergoing a rapid shift from blue-collar white ethnic (largely Polish and Italian) to black, and there had been unpleasant confrontations, although never in the library. However, the Morton Avenue branch was considered an undesirable one in which to work. It was difficult to keep good staff there because employees requested transfers to other locations almost immediately—as true for professional as for clerical workers. The physical facilities were not imposing; the building was old and the room rather drab and cheerless. Use of the branch as measured in circulation was among the lowest in the system. It occurred to Khalid that the library administration might well want to close the branch but did not dare.

Morton Avenue had employed a bright and energetic young hispanic woman as its children's librarian, and she had once told him over a cup of coffee about the formidable but not insurmountable problems of appealing to children who frequently lacked a family tradition of appreciating books. She was now gone, having moved to California, and the position had been vacant for four months. Alex Horowitz had assured him that every effort was being made to fill the position as quickly as possible, but that securing good candidates was not easy, and Khalid had no reason to disbelieve him. Nevertheless, it was also true that two branch heads had left Morton Avenue in the last two years, one to take a job at the Chicago Public Library, the other to return to school to seek a doctorate in history. Khalid had not known either one well, but he supposed he could find them if he wanted to talk to them.

As Khalid thought about all of these issues, some dark thoughts began to form in his mind. Was he truly being offered an opportunity to succeed as a manager? Or was he being programmed for certain failure, in some sort of attempt to get even with him for his previous activities?

III

INTERACTIONS WITH PATRONS

48

THE OUTRAGED PROFESSOR

Marjorie Goodlow had been dean of university libraries at Macomber University for eight years. Macomber considered itself a prestigious private university, perhaps not of Ivy League or Stanford caliber, but nevertheless very important. It courted important scholars for its faculty, and offered a whole range of doctoral programs. The university library, with a staff of fifty professionals and two million volumes, was considered an excellent collection. Funding at private universities, even at Macomber, was tight, and it had been difficult both to meet faculty expectations for collection growth and to implement new technologies. Nevertheless, continuous progress had been made, and Marjorie was generally pleased. The library was a member of the important Association of Research Libraries (ARL), and she felt she was an accepted part of the council of deans that met regularly with the president, although she rarely expressed views on topics outside the library's direct concerns. Librarians had faculty equivalent status on the campus, which meant that they all had the same privileges (including tenure and sabbatical leaves) as the teaching faculty system, but their promotion and tenure files were evaluated within the library.

This process was much fairer, Marjorie felt, and had given her a professional staff of which she was genuinely proud. It included some recognized writers in the profession and officers in state and national associations. There were, of course, some librarians who had achieved tenure during an easier and more relaxed time and who did not really pull their full weight now, but Marjorie recognized that this was true of academic departments on the campus as well. Relationships with the faculty were generally good. There were the occasional skirmishes about budgetary allocations, and she recognized that not all faculty members considered librarians their intellectual even if legal equals; but whatever sense of superiority there might be had been submerged in the Southern civility that characterized much of life on this campus. Macomber was demanding, but it had not lost its sense of style.

Marjorie's mail today contained one unusual and disturbing letter. Indeed, it was a formal letter, although it came from within the campus and such communications usually arrived as memoranda in interoffice envelopes. This letter was from Professor Klaus Augenthaler of the chemistry department. He had come from Germany to join the faculty in the fall semester just three months ago. Although Marjorie had not yet met him, she realized from the publicity surrounding the announcement of his appointment that he was one of the world's premier organic synthesis chemists and considered quite an acquisition at a university that measured much of its prestige in faculty recognition.

Professor Augenthaler's letter was brief and to the point: "Dear Dean Goodlow: I regret to have to inform you that your chemistry librarian, Monica Rogers, has been personally rude to me and impertinent to a full professor who is a member of the chemistry faculty. I expect an apology from you on behalf of the library and assurance that Miss Rogers will be properly instructed in future behavior toward faculty such as myself. Very truly yours, Dr. Klaus Augenthaler, Professor of Chemistry."

Marjorie had heard nothing about any problems in the chemistry library. Monica Rogers, she recalled, had come to Macomber six years ago from the National Bureau of Standards in Washington; Marjorie had been active in recruiting her. Monica had both an M.L.S. and a master's degree in physical chemistry. She was tenured and held the rank of associate librarian. She reported to Marjorie through Fred McGuffin, associate dean for public services. Monica had been getting along well with her fellow librarians and with the faculty and rotating chairs of the chemistry department, who served terms of three years at most, although the chemistry library materials budget had been particularly hard hit by the price increases in the scientific journal literature. Indeed, Monica was an effective and articulate—although sometimes slightly abrasive—representative and spokesperson in library staff meetings for her chemistry library and the users she served.

49

EDUCATION AND ETHICS

Gwen Martin enjoyed the opportunity to have dinner with her good friend Pam Franklin. They had met three years ago in the baggage claim area of the Centerburg airport. Both were arriving for new jobs, Gwen as reference librarian at the public library, Pam to teach English at the local high school. Both felt alone and a little scared, and they had hit it off from the beginning. They got together about once a month, and both enjoyed their friendship immensely.

Now, as they finished their coffee at the restaurant and waited for the bill, Pam had a final bit of news. "By the way, expect another flock of my juniors in the library next week. I'm about to give them the annual assignment of reading and then writing a report on a current novel of their own choosing. As before, I'll be suggesting that they might do better at the public library because the school library is not big on current fiction." Gwen, who had gone through this process with two earlier generations of Pam's junior students, nevertheless appreciated being alerted. It hadn't been and shouldn't be a problem. The public library had an adequate if not grandiose collection budget, and like many public libraries tried to stock the current novels that were in vogue. While the best sellers were usually impossible to get for about six months, after that they were available, and some excellent books not plugged on the afternoon talk shows were always on the shelves. Pam let her juniors read and report on whatever they liked, and up to now at least, there had been no problems either for the library or the school board. High school students had always been allowed full access to all library materials, and Gwen was not going to invent any problems.

And so, one by one, as predicted, over the next few days the juniors trickled in. Some were of course regular users of the library, and knew what to do for themselves; others headed to the reference desk to seek advice and counsel from Gwen. Eventually everybody had settled upon a book to read and analyze. Gwen had to smile at the thought that for some of them, brevity seemed a more important feature than author, subject, or style of writing.

The number of juniors coming in for this assignment had subsided and, Gwen thought, the class had finished selecting their books, when Tony LoMassimo appeared. He looked tall enough to be a basketball player and large enough to be a football player, but Gwen didn't follow local high school sports. She did not recall having seen Tony before, but he identified himself through his library card, although that was hardly necessary to get reference help, and asked exactly what the others had asked. It occurred to Gwen that he was rather late getting started, but as he hadn't specifically mentioned a course assignment or a due date she decided not to bring it up. She directed Tony to the appropriate sections of the library shelves. There was still a good collection, and Gwen remembered that there were a couple of sports novels. She made herself a mental bet that he would pick one of these. She liked playing these little mental games, and they did no harm.

She was not expecting another visit from Tony, and therefore his next request surprised her. Since there were so many books, were there any book reviews, particularly good, detailed ones, that he could consult before making his final selection? The library had a subscription to the Sunday *New York Times,* and when Tony was shown the book review section he was extremely grateful and took a stack of them to a table in the corner. Gwen was busy with telephone calls and other patrons, but she noticed that Tony made several trips to the self-service photocopy machine. She also noticed when he left the library about thirty minutes later. He did not check out any books.

50

A VISIT FROM BELOW THE SEA

Taking the post as library director at Palmetto State University eight years ago had seemed like the perfect opportunity for Mary Elizabeth Corrigan. At the age of 45, she had been working in academic libraries for over twenty years, since graduation from library school, and had worked her way up to assistant director for technical services at a respectable state A & M university. Her ambitions, she realized, were limited. She had neither the political acumen nor the drive to aim for an Association of Research Libraries (ARL) directorship, and she also realized that she would never be a prolific author and scholar.

Palmetto State had seemed like the perfect place at which to spend the next eighteen to twenty years and then retire. Located near some fabulous Florida beaches, and more noted for the prowess of its athletic teams than for its academic prestige, Palmetto was what used to be called a "country club school." Its students tended to be more affluent than intellectual, and their dedication to parties exceeded their commitment to education. There were graduate programs, but these were heavily populated by overseas students from countries where the desire for warm weather was greatest. As is usually the case, the philosophy of the school attracted a faculty who accepted that philosophy. Palmetto's faculty members were easygoing, and made as few demands on the library as on their students. Taking the post with an eye toward a future retirement location and a home for her widowed mother, Mary Elizabeth inherited a library staff with similar value systems. She had noted quickly that there was virtually no turnover except for death or retirement, and indeed, her predecessor had gracefully retired and faded from the scene. Hiring new young graduates when such opportunities arose provided little difficulty. Palmetto's salaries were low, but the style of life was great, and somehow the job notices attracted enough candidates ready to buy into the value system.

The library building was beautiful, a gleaming white structure facing a lawn that led to a beach, and while the collection was no great accomplishment it satisfied the faculty and had caused no problems with regional accreditation teams. As faculty asked for books or journals, the library had no difficulty in meeting their requests. The collection development officer had left for an ARL institution a year after Mary Elizabeth's arrival and Mary Elizabeth had felt no need to replace her. She allowed the subject librarians among her staff of thirty-five professionals to make selections in cooperation with the faculty, and the system worked just fine. The library had automated circulation and processing functions by buying into a proven existing system. It all worked satisfactorily, and the faculty never complained. The state legislature, like so many others, was more concerned with the accomplishments of the athletic teams, and certainly caused no problems.

This had all begun to change when Mortimer Birnbaum was named to the presidency eighteen months ago. Birnbaum had argued that academic and athletic excellence were not incompatible; his role models were schools like Michigan and UCLA. He was a mesmerizing and dynamic speaker, who had clearly converted some important people. In the first year after his arrival, Birnbaum had caused the library no trouble; indeed, he still hadn't to this day. A sociologist with an impressive research and administrative record, Birnbaum seemed to understand the importance of library collections but not necessarily of librarians. The building was considered adequate for at least ten years of future growth, but Birnbaum had stated early on that improving library collections was one of his first priorities. He did not talk about the qualifications of the librarians, and Mary Elizabeth, who had no plans for staff upgrading and indeed saw potential risks for herself in such a priority, had not broached the question. If the library needed to buy more materials, Birnbaum seemed amenable to finding the money. If all of this had implications in regard to the size or quality of the staff, it seemed not to have occurred to Birnbaum.

Nevertheless, as Birnbaum's new faculty recruits began arriving on campus, Mary Elizabeth began to feel increasingly uneasy. She should probably do something, but what? Today's appointment with Dr. Wendell Corson had probably been an extreme example, but nevertheless just an extension of the developing pattern. Dr. Corson had called before lunch, and apologizing for the short notice, asked if he could see her for a few minutes that afternoon before he had to leave for the airport. Elizabeth had time on her schedule, and she welcomed Dr. Corson graciously, wondering who he was and what he wanted. She didn't have long to wait.

He was currently a faculty member at the Scripps Institution for Oceanography at La Jolla, California, but would be coming to Palmetto in seven months to set up what was planned to be a major East Coast research facility for the study of the oceans. President Birnbaum would be making the announcement in about two weeks, but although this information was still sensitive, Corson assumed that the library director already knew. She let the statement pass without comment.

"My discussions with President Birnbaum and the board have concentrated almost exclusively on issues of funding, buildings, laboratory equipment, and staff," Corson continued. "At the same time the president and I are both aware of the fact that the library has very little of the research materials needed to support this new program. Nor would we expect that it now would. Nevertheless, time is quite urgent if we are to make a proper start in September. I will be making several more trips here before September, but most of my time will be spent in California finishing my work there, selling my house, and getting my family ready for the move. I've taken the liberty of compiling a list of about 150 journal titles and 500 monographs that would comprise a starting nucleus for our work. Obviously, this is just the beginning. I have indicated the number of back years required for each title. I understand that there may be some difficulty in obtaining some of these, but I'm sure you librarians have your ways. In any case President Birnbaum has assured me that the library has always been very cooperative and authorized me to tell you that he would be glad to discuss with you any problems this might raise.

"I apologize for the abruptness of this visit, but I have a plane to catch. Here is my card with my La Jolla phone number. Please call me if you have any questions or concerns. I hope that at least most of this material can be in place and available by September."

After Corson left, Mary Elizabeth glanced at the list of materials he had given her. The journal titles were almost all new for this library, and considering the total lack of emphasis on oceanography until now this was no surprise. She felt equally certain that virtually all of the monographs would be new for the collection as well.

51
ONE DIVIDED BY TWO EQUALS ONE

School librarian Harriet Morrison did not find the statements by the assistant superintendent of schools for administration and personnel particularly surprising. She knew about the financial straits of the school district brought about by the relocation of the community's largest industrial tax payer. School enrollment had also been flat, perhaps even suffered a slight decline. All teachers (and Harriet was of course a member of the union) understood that under the contract the school board could cut personnel levels most easily through attrition. However, the contract also had language concerning class size, and classroom teaching positions were therefore not easy to cut. Harriet was librarian at the Grove Junior High School. Faith Binkley, the librarian at the other junior high school, Pleasant Ridge, had just retired. Harriet did not want to think ill of her, but Faith had never impressed her as a professional. She was stern and formidable, and had paid little attention to the innovative ideas presented in the literature and at meetings. Teachers and parents who were familiar with both junior high school libraries had told Harriet how much more effective and useful her library was. She had done a good job despite financial difficulties, and she felt she had a right to be pleased.

The assistant superintendent had explained that Faith would not be replaced, as indeed several other individuals, particularly in nonclassroom service areas, would not be replaced. Harriet would in the future be supervising both junior high libraries, splitting time between the two. He realized that this would be difficult, but he also had confidence in her ability to cope and to improvise during these difficult times. They would try to provide her with some additional support staff assistance, but at this point he couldn't promise. The materials budgets, already diluted by inflation, would be kept at their present fixed dollar levels, at least for the present.

The assistant superintendent had one final point to make, and although they were alone in his office he dropped his voice conspiratorily. "These cuts and adjustments, which I am sure you understand are absolutely necessary, could create a good deal of concern and anxiety in the community, particularly among some of the more actively involved parents. It is absolutely essential that we approach these changes with a sense of confidence. We must assure the parents that educational services to their children will not suffer. And I am certain that, with the dedicated group of professionals we have here, they won't."

Harriet, who knew that it took all her full-time energies and some of her evenings and weekends to provide Grove with the innovative programs of which she was so proud, did not have the vaguest idea how to split her time between two schools without having at least the Grove students suffer. Pleasant Ridge students might even benefit, if half of a Harriet Morrison was preferable to a full-time Faith Binkley; if that sounded smug she couldn't help it, because she thought it was true. In any case, Harriet decided that worrying about this complex problem could wait until tomorrow, and that she needed to cheer herself up with a nice dinner in her favorite restaurant.

Harriet had just returned from the salad bar when Doreen Carmichael came over to her table. Doreen was president of the Grove PTA, and an articulate if sometimes combative figure at school-board meetings. Harriet got along with Doreen just fine, and the Carmichaels' daughter Judy was an excellent student aide in the library. "May I talk to you for a second?" Doreen asked, and without waiting for an answer sat down in the booth opposite Harriet. "We've heard disturbing rumors about what those characters in the school administration are likely to pull, and I'm particularly bothered by the suggestion that they will make no attempt to replace librarians or art and music teachers as they resign or retire. As though those things weren't important! They're the essence of quality education for our children! We've heard that the Pleasant Ridge librarian has retired, and we're obviously worried about what this means if they don't replace her. We're prepared to fight to keep you as a full-time librarian at Grove if they have any idea of splitting your time, and if that is suggested I want you to tell me right away. I will also need you to tell me what sort of impact on library service for the students such a move would have. Pretty drastic, I would think, but if I know those people in the administration building, they'll try to con us into thinking none at all. In any case, you're the one who would really know."

Harriet realized that Doreen had said all of this with one breath, or at least she hadn't seemed to stop to take one. However, now Doreen had stopped and was sitting there, looking at Harriet and waiting for an answer.

52

WHEN IS A COST NOT A COST?

Heather Freeman faced a dilemma. What was her responsibility and loyalty to direct instructions from her boss when following them might conflict with her perception of what would best serve the corporation? Heather had been library manager of Universal Technologies for over eight years. She had put together a strong group of six professional and eight nonprofessional staff members, and reaction to library services from the scientists, engineers, economists, and marketing people who used the library had been positive. She had developed services, and in particular had expanded reference services, especially in areas of data-base searching. Once offered, this library service had really taken off. Her staff had grown, specifically in the recruitment of librarians with on-line search skills and subject degrees that made for high-quality searchers. Universal paid good salaries, making recruitment for these specialized skills possible.

Fred Andersen's appointment as director of corporate services, the department to which the library reported, had coincided with a downturn in Universal's fortunes. The situation was not catastrophic but nevertheless quite a change from years of uninterrupted growth and increasing profitability. Fred was a long-term company employee, and Heather recognized that it was longevity and not intuitive brilliance that had characterized his career at Universal. Fred was a far cry from Heather's former boss, but she realized that in the real world one did not get to select one's boss. She had attempted to meet Fred's management style more than halfway, and indeed Fred was always friendly and cordial toward her.

Nevertheless, Fred Andersen had determined early during this time of reduced profitability that his contribution, and that of the units that reported to him, would be to lower operating costs. There had been no layoffs, because that was not yet the Universal style, but the staffing increases had stopped immediately, and as positions became vacant through resignation or retirement Fred had instituted a policy of eliminating them. In fairness, Fred had done this not just to the library but to all of his subordinate units. It was clearly his goal to build his corporate reputation, which was not all that impressive, on cost-cutting.

All this had hit Heather pretty hard, particularly in the area of on-line literature searching, because she had endured two sudden professional resignations that Fred had refused to allow her to replace. And yet demand for library services, particularly in this area, had not abated. Indeed, it had grown. When Heather discussed this concern with Andersen, his solution was simple. Data-base searches did not have to be done by the library staff, they could be done by the actual user. The staff would run some training seminars, and vendors could be brought in on a one-time basis to run others. Little by little, the library staff could get out of the literature-searching business except under the most unusual circumstances. Not only would the library save on time and effort, but the cost of machine time, which had been allocated to requesting departments but never accurately, would now simply accrue to the departments that wanted to do the search.

Heather had qualms about the procedure, but she did not want to appear immediately negative in her attitude toward her new boss so she had gone along with it. Some of the users were annoyed at the news that henceforth they were to do their own data-base searching; others accepted it without any rancor. Some individuals, faced with the alternative of having their own searches or none at all, chose the latter, and the use of data bases dropped sharply. Fred Andersen took this news as a vindication of his strategy. Obviously, he concluded, those unwilling to do their own literature searches had never needed them in the first place, and he reported this "savings" in his management report.

Heather considered this conclusion simplistic if not totally wrong. She was concerned that the failure to undertake literature searches might be less because of a lack of need and more because of the inconvenience. How many *needed* searches were now not being done, and how many technical and business decisions might now be made incompletely or even incorrectly? Fred Andersen did not consider this an issue, and others in the corporate management chain had not even thought about it.

However, Heather was even more concerned with a new problem about which she was quite certain. Those users who *were* doing their own literature searches were now often doing poorly worded searches, were searching wrong and obsolete data bases when better ones existed, and were spending far more time in the process than a competent librarian–searcher would have. None of this concerned Fred Andersen, because such inefficiencies, if they were real, would not reflect in his budget. Heather's conscience was not so easily assuaged. She was the corporate information professional, and the corporation's money, as she saw it, was being wasted in two very dangerous ways: first, in that needed searches were not being done at all and decisions therefore made without complete background; and second, that many of the searches being done were being done badly and inefficiently.

Heather's eight years at Universal had not been idly spent. She knew both the president and the vice-president for finance rather well, and the library had served them in the past.

53
DESELECTION IN THE PERIODICALS BUDGET

Library director Derek Brownlow turned off the light in his office, locked the door, and went home. It was after 11 P.M. and after looking at all the alternatives he had made his decision. The problems of escalating periodical prices obviously did not plague his institution alone. To the best of his reckoning, the huge annual price increases went back at least eighteen years, or ten years before his assumption of the directorship. For the last eight years he had done what his predecessor, and indeed most ARL directors, had done. He had shifted funds from other parts of the materials budget, he had deferred and ultimately canceled other library initiatives, and he had literally begged the university administration for additional materials funds, even though he knew that this destroyed his chances of getting money for other priorities. His library had worked with others in establishing consortiums and networks under which ownership of lesser-used journals was assigned to one member, despite the fact that both the publishers and the faculty had objected. He had asked the library staff to make judicious cuts in titles that were used less often or used primarily by the staff rather than the faculty. Everybody else had done this as well.

Two weeks ago he had received, through his head of serials, the projection from the subscription agency that the present university subscription list, already battered and bruised and reduced in almost all cases to one systemwide copy per periodical, would increase in price an average of 19.5 percent with smaller increases in domestic and larger in foreign titles, and of course particularly large increases in the physical sciences. The projection, he knew from past reports, was probably accurate at least plus or minus 1 percent.

He had immediately scheduled a meeting with the university president. The president was sorry, but refused to promise anything beyond the 5 percent budget increase that would be available through state funding and tuition increases. The university simply had too many other priorities, including faculty salaries, which of course included librarian salaries. The president had suggested, but had not demanded, that the library reallocate resources from other areas to the periodicals budget. When Derek reminded the president that this had been done before, he acknowledged that this was true. "Do whatever you can to deal with this issue in the least traumatic manner" was all the president had to offer.

The library staff meeting two days ago was probably the most emotional ever, at least in this university. Derek had reported his conversation with the president and the president's comments. He asked for suggestions from the assembled group. At first there was nothing to be said, but then the accumulated frustration broke free. They refused to put aside other priorities to salvage the serials budget yet one more time. They had cut, and cut. They had endured faculty anger, and disillusionment and charges of betrayal from their own staff members. There was simply nothing else they could do. The president simply had to be persuaded to furnish the money. Several librarians had cried.

Derek Brownlow was grateful that at least their frustration and anger had not turned on one another, or on him. And yet he also knew that the president would not or could not furnish additional dollars—unless, just perhaps, he forced the president's hand. It was about this that he had just made a decision.

Periodical subscriptions assigned directly to one of the fifteen branches were already coded to the department or school that housed the branch and were under the control of the branch librarians. Main library subscriptions fell into areas of responsibility of subject specialists, and Derek felt quite sure that anything left over could also be assigned, arbitrarily by classification number if necessary. He was grateful that the competition for fund allocations, which had been fierce, had never turned bitter or personally ugly. He would not risk it now, and he would not ask his staff to make more traumatic decisions.

His plan was simply to delegate, or perhaps abdicate, the decisions of what to keep and renew to the cognizant schools and departments. He would furnish them with a list of titles assigned to them, with current prices, projected prices, and totals for both. He would tell each group to submit a list that reflected no more than a 5 percent increase over this year's total; he would tell them that he recognized that this was tougher on some units than on others, but that he held them responsible for any failure to control the publication process in their own discipline. If units failed to comply either by failing to return the list or to meet the targets, the library would do it through a process of random deselection not unlike a lottery.

He knew that would certainly get their attention. They might comply, but it was just as likely that all hell would break loose. If that happened, would the president "find" more money? Would they all band together to fire Derek? He was, to his own surprise, quite calm at the prospect. Perhaps he had just battled too long and was too tired. He managed a chuckle at the thought that if they fired him, it still wouldn't solve what he saw as the classic problem of the irresistible force and the immovable object.

54

THE USE OF VOLUNTEERS IN THE SCHOOL LIBRARY

Florence Galloway, supervisor of media services for the Washington County School District, was having one of her periodic planning and review sessions with Dr. Alonzo Hooker, superintendent of schools. Florence had planning and coordinating responsibilities for all the school librarians (or media specialists) in the school district, although nominally they reported to the principal of their school. She was entrusted with recruitment and initial hiring recommendations, and with making overall policy suggestions for school library matters.

Although Florence and Dr. Hooker always got along well and he seemed to have a respect for her views and judgments, of late the discussions had been less pleasant. Florence Galloway realized that this wasn't all Alonzo Hooker's fault. Over the last five years there had been cuts in the school budget from a shrinking tax base and a declining school population. Several schools had been closed and consolidated. At the same time, Washington County, which was in a heavily blue-collar area of the state, had a militant teacher's union, and there had been several work stoppages and threats of others. Although Florence was in one sense a beneficiary of labor negotiations, as a supervisor she was not a union member; she guessed that the school board acting on Dr. Hooker's recommendations had probably granted more of a salary increase in the last contract than it could afford.

Teacher numbers had started to decline, primarily through attrition, reflecting both budgetary and enrollment realities. In schools that once had six fifth-grade teachers and now had only four, that was bad enough. However, how do you reduce the number of librarians when there is only one in a school to begin with?

The Washington County approach, hardly atypical, had been to double up assignments. School media specialists now routinely supervised two school libraries, and in some cases three. It led to poorer service, shorter hours, and problems that could only get worse. Some of the more militant PTA groups in schools especially affected had begun to make noises about the quality of school library service. There was a school board election coming up in five months, and Florence was certain that Alonzo Hooker was under considerable pressure.

Yet despite all of this, they were now discussing a further shrinkage in the population of school media specialists. Two of the best ones had submitted their resignations at the end of the school year. They had both cited personal reasons, but Florence knew that as much had to do with overwork and burnout. Those fortunate enough to have accredited M.L.S. degrees as well as certification were, in other school districts as well as this one, opting for transfers to other kinds of libraries. And yet Florence was hearing from Alonzo Hooker that in a way this represented an opportunity to cut back further without inflicting the pain of layoffs and terminations. Florence Galloway, who had said all of this before to little effect, repeated all the reasons why a further dilution in the number of school media specialists was unthinkable. She emphasized that not only would there be an impact on the quality of educational services, but that it would stoke further resentments on the part of parent groups.

Alonzo Hooker let her finish her remarks without interruption, and then he spoke. "There is another way, Florence, and I wanted to have your reaction to this idea. I have been given to understand that among the parents in this school district are quite a few who have education in school librarianship and media services. A number even earned certification as school librarians and media specialists here and in other states. These would have to be brought up to date, but I am sure we could arrange this. Given the financial pressures as well as the real problems in staffing our school media centers, I am confident that a campaign to solicit volunteers would bring out quite a few—and I mean *qualified* volunteers who know something about running a school library, who would be willing to come in for perhaps as much as ten hours or more a week to help run the libraries in the schools their own children attend.

"What do you think about the idea of recruiting some of these people—of tapping this potential to help with our problems? I've checked with the officers of the teacher's union. As long as these people did not undertake classroom instruction and concentrated simply on the business end of running and organizing libraries—you know, selecting and ordering material, getting it ready for use by the teachers and pupils—the union would not object, knowing that they would not replace any union jobs. They would want assurance that in the event of a financial turnaround we would go back to hiring real school librarians, but that likelihood for Washington County is so remote that I'm perfectly willing to make that commitment. What do you think?"

55

ADVICE FROM THE MIDDLE SCHOOL USERS

Greta Lagerquist had established the student advisory committee from the very beginning of her service as media specialist at Davey Crockett Middle School. Some teachers had made snide remarks about her need to get advice from middle schoolers about how to run the library, but other teachers had been quite supportive, and the principal had raised no objection. The establishment of the committee was now old news in any case, and nobody seemed to notice any more. The group was to a large extent self-selecting, involving some of the brightest and most innovative students in the school. It was also largely self-perpetuating. Students tended to become members in their first year, and remain until they graduated to high school or transferred to another school. They were caring library users who took their responsibilities seriously. High school librarians had commented on what a superior group of library users the "graduates" of Greta's program were, and she was pleased.

She went to great pains to make the students feel that they were making a real contribution, and she never ridiculed their suggestions. In reality, that wasn't necessary because their suggestions often made a lot of sense. On many occasions, looking at an issue with the eyes of library users, they could see problems and solutions she did not even notice. The committee met monthly for an hour after the last class on the third Wednesday of the month, and Greta looked forward to the experience.

Despite the success of the committee, all was not well in the use of the media center. Some students never or hardly ever used it at all, others only when literally forced to by an assignment. Greta knew that to some extent a number of the teachers were to blame, because they still used media center assignments as a form of threat or of punishment. Students reacted accordingly. At last month's meeting Greta had asked the committee to give some thought to ideas for making the media center a more pleasant and inviting place. She expected suggestions about decorations, displays, and perhaps special promotions.

She got all of these, and some of them very good, but she got more from Jennifer Bentley. Jenny was a natural student leader, who combined intelligence with popularity. Greta was glad she was also interested in libraries.

"I know the role of libraries in support of teaching and to encourage reading on our own," Jenny began. "All of that is great, but it isn't going to work if you don't get the students in here, or if they treat coming in like going to the dentist. I think you should stock some recreational videos, and maybe even some Nintendo™ games, and let students check them out, maybe over the weekend. Perhaps you can even tie in taking this stuff out to taking out other materials along with it."

Jenny's suggestion was received enthusiastically by her fellow students. Even Greta felt pulled into the excitement. She smiled at the simple charm of Jenny's explanation that Nintendo games were good for education because they developed hand–eye coordination.

56

A PROBLEM WITH VANDALISM

Like just about any high school library, Indian Springs had some problems with theft. Usually it was recent issues of sports magazines, sometimes a photography magazine with some suggestive pictures, occasionally a book. The situation was reasonably well in hand. The library, or school media center as it was called, had turnstiles installed beside the circulation desk, and students had to pass through them as they left. Librarian Paula Kenton estimated the loss through theft at about $20 to $30 per month. It was a "cost of business" they could live with; it did not warrant the implementation of any closer scrutiny or searches, which would certainly negate the warm and friendly impression that Paula had worked so hard to create.

The problem with computer readable information discs' (CD/ROM) disappearance was something else. Paula had been very proud and pleased when she had been able to institute the use of discs in the media center. Not only did it provide access to a new broad range of information products and services, but learning how to use CD/ROM was, she thought, a very important part of bibliographic instruction and preparation for the information world beyond high school, in college, or in the workplace. CD/ROMs were expensive, ranging in price from $50 and $100 to $500 or $600. However, she had slowly and carefully built this part of the service. Students enjoyed the new options, and teacher reaction had been very positive.

She had not expected any thefts of these discs, because they could not really be used except on special equipment that individual students usually did not have. Besides, unlike sports magazines and photographs, these were research tools, rather dry and pedantic and certainly not used for fun. And yet Paula had to face the reality that these discs were disappearing at an alarming rate. She had not attempted any detailed inventory, but there had been a number of situations in which a disc was nowhere to be found despite an extensive search. Paula had to conclude, reluctantly, that some of these discs were just being stolen. What disturbed her even more was the realization that these were simply acts of spite or vandalism.

She realized she had a problem. These discs were too expensive to be replaced either on a casual or even a planned basis, and if the principal learned of the problem he might well forbid further disc purchases. Paula also realized that it was much easier to hide a disc in one's clothes than a book or a magazine.

57

HELPING LOVE ALONG

The Universal Aerospace Company Technical Information Center, which Neil Baumgarten directed, subscribed, as might be expected, to a considerable number of international periodicals. Many of these, particularly the news magazines, were received via air mail. Of the TIC's 600 periodical titles, about 150 were international. Harriet Bogard supervised the process of receiving the issues, logging them into the computer system, and then developing routing lists for the multiple copies. Neil normally had little contact with Harriet, unless it was a problem involving missing issues that the publisher refused to furnish or some concern with the bindery. None of this happened often, and Neil felt that this part of the operation was well in hand.

When Harriet knocked and entered his office, she was smiling; that reassured him so he smiled back. "I thought you'd like to see this," Harriet said. "I've tried to put the package back together just the way it was when Julia Franken, who opened it, brought it to me." It was the latest issue of *Aerospace Weekly,* a British business publication read regularly by a significant number of Universal's executives and managers. Between the cover and the first page of the rolled-up journal was an envelope, and when he opened the envelope to extract the letter a snapshot also fell out. He read the letter.

> "Dear librarian: My name is Christine Andrews, and I work in the shipping department of this magazine. I am 22 years old and single. I've always like American men, although I don't get to meet too many here in Manchester. I would really appreciate it if you could show this letter to any nice single American engineers who might be interested in starting a correspondence with me. Who knows what it might lead to? I've enclosed a picture for you to show them, and my friends say I am not bad-looking. I like sports, the cinema, dancing, and just about any of the things a girl my age might like. I'm hoping that you will help me, by selecting whom you give this to. I don't want to get involved with any married men, because I can get plenty of those to make a pass at me here. However, any nice single engineers up to about 30 would be fine. They don't have to be tall (although I'm pretty tall, also blonde) and they don't have to be good-looking. My friends tell me that there are lots of single professionals working in companies like yours. There are hardly any in ours. Thanks for your help. Sincerely, Chris Andrews."

The picture was not very good, but from the snapshot of the smiling young girl wearing a sweatshirt and shorts and sitting on a bicycle, Neil would certainly agree that Christine Andrews (assuming it was a picture of Christine Andrews) was quite pretty.

58
THIS IS THE YEAR FOR CHAUCER

As library director of North Suburban Community College, Salvatore Callini knew exactly what the college was and what it was not. It was a very large institution with more than 25,000 students. Almost all of the courses were in the evening, and virtually all of the students were part-timers who attended classes after working all day. Sal had not seen any official statistics on graduation rates or on transfers to nearby universities, but he was quite sure that both were low. Nevertheless, institutions like North Suburban Community College performed an important role for those who were unable, for financial or even academic reasons, to enroll in one of the more prestigious colleges or universities in the area. The North Suburban library was always crowded, particularly in the evenings and on weekends. Part of this was because the library was too small and underfunded, part because many (if not all) the students worked hard, seeing this as their one and perhaps last chance at education and upward mobility.

The faculty, like the librarians, worked under great pressures. Classes were large, and the faculty were required to teach at least three and sometimes four sections per semester. North Suburban's open admission system, under which any resident of the state who was a high school graduate or possessed equivalent credentials could enroll, made it difficult to impose any sort of across-the-board standards. But in spite of all the handicaps, there were students who grew and bloomed; it was they who made it all worthwhile to Sal Callini, who had steadfastly refused to explore opportunities to apply for posts in more traditional academic settings. Callini assumed that those who taught at North Suburban shared this value system. There were many faculty members, some full-time and many part-time, whom Sal knew to be as dedicated as he was. Whatever dreams of academic distinction they might once have harbored had been shelved, and Sal assumed that as in his own case, it was to pursue this greater good.

That is why the letter from Professor Webster Goodnight of the English department had come as such a great surprise. Without any preamble Goodnight had submitted a list of forty-seven books, all works by and about Chaucer, that he stated had to be acquired and processed in time for the next fall semester. Callini did not know Goodnight personally, but he knew that whatever Chaucer material was covered in the general literature-survey courses dealing with the time period was handled quite adequately by the collection they already had. Goodnight was asking not only for commentaries in several languages, but also for editions that included Chaucer's writings in the original English. Sal could not even begin to guess as to what percentage of these books was even available in print, but he wasn't about to start that exercise. North Suburban had no honors courses in English, let alone graduate programs, and its faculty were not scholars but teachers who occasionally wrote articles and book reviews. An extensive Chaucer collection did not fit the institution's mission. Surely there had been some sort of mistake.

He had responded to Professor Goodnight, stating his observations and concerns and suggesting a meeting in which they could discuss these issues. Professor Goodnight's response was curt and direct to the point of rudeness. He said that whether Callini realized it or not, he, Goodnight, was an acknowledged scholar in Chaucerian literature. He needed these works for his own research, and for advanced classes he was planning to teach. The list was brief and quite reasonable, and he saw no reason to discuss it.

Sal decided he'd better talk to Walter Rappoport, longtime chairman of the English department. They had known each for better than fifteen years. Rappoport, who was probably nearing retirement age and who to Sal's recollection had been at North Suburban for at least twenty-five years, was an amiable and easygoing fellow; he and Sal Callini had always had a good relationship. Sal asked if they could get together to discuss a problem with one of the English department faculty members, and Walt suggested that they meet for a drink before heading home that evening.

Sal showed Rappoport the correspondence, which the department chairman read and returned without comment. Sal started to launch into his explanation of why he considered the request totally unreasonable, but Walt waved him into silence. "You don't have to convince me, Sal. I know how silly all of this seems. However, I also know what's behind it and I think I'd better tell you. Web Goodnight is a dedicated teacher and has always had promise as a scholar. He received his doctorate from Yale twelve years ago, and despite the fact that his dissertation was quite favorably received, jobs in major English departments then as now were not easy to come by. Goodnight accepted his post here as a temporary expedient, planning at the appropriate time to move on to bigger and better things. For the first five years here, Goodnight was relatively patient, but he's become increasingly restless. I know he's applied for a lot of positions, because I've been contacted with regard to many of them. The problem is that Web is good but not *that* good, and the longer he stays here the more stigmatized he becomes. I think this has finally dawned on him, but I think the last straw was last month when his own dissertation advisor at Yale didn't even include him in the short list of people to be interviewed."

Rappoport took a long swig of his Scotch and soda and looked directly at Sal. "Sal, I know this may all seem like nonsense, but Goodnight is going through an identity crisis in which he is trying to salvage his own self-esteem. We obviously don't need a Chaucer collection here, although Goodnight would probably made a pretty good pass at doing some serious research. However, he could do that with the material at the state university. What he's trying to do is replicate as much as possible the collection he might have had at Yale, as sort of a consolation prize. He's not thinking very clearly right now, but he's a good man and a good teacher, and in time he will accept his place in the educational establishment, as I have and as I assume you have. I know you can't buy all this stuff, Sal, and I don't expect you to. But buy what you can, to help salvage this fellow's dignity. I'll really appreciate it."

59
I WANT MY FAVORITE REFERENCE LIBRARIAN

The staff meeting of department heads had gone pretty much on schedule, and they had come to the end of the formal agenda. Public library director Ernestina Hernandez said, really as a formality and out of habit, "Is there any new business?" There were the usual announcements about guest speakers and reminders about the picnic but never anything of substance. If there were real agenda items of importance her department heads knew she wanted to be briefed about the issues before the meeting.

Today, however, was different. Malcolm Hubbell, head of reference, cleared his throat, looked around the room a little apprehensively, and then spoke. Ernestina did not feel really comfortable with Malcolm, whom she did not consider an imaginative or inspiring leader and who never seemed to have any ideas to contribute. However, he did his job well enough, and, perhaps by luck, he had a number of excellent reference librarians. Malcolm had been at the library in his present post before Ernestina had been hired, and there certainly were no grounds for either demoting or firing him. Sometimes you just took what you got.

Hubbell spoke. "I didn't put this on the agenda because I wasn't sure this was the appropriate place to bring it up. Maybe you would have preferred that I discuss this with you privately. But anyway, here goes. You all know that our telephone reference service, which is excellent if I do say so myself, is staffed on a rotating basis by all the reference librarians. The work involves pressure, and some like it better than others, but I have always felt it was fair to distribute this responsibility evenly. The reference librarians also have other responsibilities, including annotations, selection, and some ongoing literature searches, and all of this provides a useful mix. Certainly none of the reference librarians has ever complained about the arrangement, although of course sometimes there are problems about the schedule."

Ernestina Hernandez wished he would get to the point. She had a luncheon appointment. Finally Malcolm did. "The people who call the library with reference questions obviously get whoever is scheduled to answer the phone. For most of the callers it doesn't make any difference, because they don't know one librarian from another. However, there are some callers, particularly from the business community, who have developed favorites. They ask for a reference librarian by name, and when they are told that this person isn't on duty they ask either when he or she will be on the desk or that the reference librarian call them back. Some of the people to whom these callers won't give their questions may be a little upset, and in any case it tends to undermine my own strategy for assigning these responsibilities evenly. It's obviously true, here as anywhere, that some reference librarians are better than others, and that some know some subject fields better than others. I don't see any point in discussing that here. However, our library *has* no subject departments, and all our reference librarians are expected to be generalists, fielding questions initially and asking one another for help when they need it. I just wondered if you, Ernestina, or any of the others might have some suggestions on how to deal with these stubborn callers without alienating them and without upsetting the system?"

60
TO SERVE THE WILL OF GOD

Albert Millgran's first three days as director of the Cedartown Public Library had been hectic but also enjoyable. He had met the three assistant directors, the personnel librarian, his office staff, and all of the professional librarians. The board of trustees had an informal reception for him at the chairwoman's house. He had paid a courtesy call on the mayor, who had been rather vague but at least pleasant; and he had also met with the director of the city budget agency, who had briefed him on forms and procedures. It was Millgran's impression, as indeed it had been during his interview visit, that the Cedartown Public Library was basically a smoothly functioning organization. There were problems, of course, particularly financial problems, but no real and immediate crises. His predecessor had died in his sleep five months earlier, a well-loved and mourned figure in the community. The assistant directors had held down the fort until Millgran was selected and started work. He had previously been assistant director at New City Public Library; New City was larger, but Millgran had felt ready for a directorship of his own.

He now began the process of sorting the mail that his secretary had set aside as being less urgent. Betty Sue Roberts, who seemed cheerful and efficient, had told him it contained the usual invitations from banks and realtors, as well as welcoming letters from the various civic clubs. He knew that he would have to decide which to join and which to concentrate on, because public image was important.

The letters were pretty much just as Betty Sue had described, except one, which he found troubling. It was brief and friendly, but he read it three times to be sure about it. It was from Dr. Robert Kingford—Pastor of the Cedartown True Gospel Church, according to the printed letterhead. It said:

> "Dear Mr. Millgran. As the pastor and spiritual leader of Cedartown's largest fundamentalist church, I want to extend an especial welcome

to you as a new resident of this community. I do not know your religious convictions, but I would like to extend an invitation to join us on any Sunday morning for our worship service. I hope that you will find it in your heart to accept this invitation. However, even if you are of a different persuasion I am anxious to make your acquaintance, so that we can discuss effective ways in which we can all further God's work. Please call me when you have settled in sufficiently. I would like to suggest lunch at one of our fine downtown restaurants, since our church and library are only about two blocks apart. Yours in Christ, Robert Kingford, Ph.D."

After the third reading of the letter Millgran dropped it back on his desk. He gave a deep sigh and muttered to himself, "Oh boy, I didn't need this."

61

I DON'T WANT MY CHILD TO BRING HOME DIRTY BOOKS

Library director Edna Mulloy could see that Mrs. Lindstrom was genuinely angry. She had literally barged into her office without an appointment (Edna had instructed her secretary not to make an issue when individuals refused to abide by the request that they make an appointment), and she had waved a copy of a recently published romance novel under Edna's nose. "I don't want my ten-year-old daughter reading this junk! That's not why I send her to the library and not why I pay taxes!"

Edna had no particular fondness for romance novels either, but that wasn't the point. She had never seen Mrs. Lindstrom before, although she did know the ten-year-old in question. Jennifer Lindstrom practically haunted the library on a daily basis. She was a voracious reader, who had won several summer reading program prizes. Edna surmised that at this point Jennifer, with a bright child's curiosity, had just been adventuring. Making a big issue of this book was probably a bad tactic for Mrs. Lindstrom if she was trying to influence Jenny's reading habits, but that wasn't the point, either. At least Mrs. Lindstrom had not brought Jennifer to this confrontational meeting.

"Are you telling me that one of our librarians recommended that Jennifer read this book?" Edna began patiently. She was sure of the answer, but it was important to set the record straight.

"No, I'm not saying that. I'm just concerned that children can wander around in the library reading anything. I'm not a censor, but I draw the line at my child's reading this smutty stuff." Edna wondered how much of the book Mrs. Lindstrom had read. She herself was no expert on romance novels, but she knew that they tended to be more suggestive than graphic.

Edna began again. "We would be delighted to have one of the librarians help Jennifer in her book selection if she would like to have help. As you know, Jennifer is a very active reader, and we want to keep her interest alive. Or if you prefer, you might either instruct Jenny on what you would like her to read. Even better, come with her to the library to help form her reading habits. However, we have no rules concerning access to any part of the collection for any of our patrons. Such rules would be just about impossible to enforce, and they would probably be illegal. The American Library Association has strongly urged that such limitations not be put into place. As a parent you obviously have the right to instruct Jennifer about your value system, and I have invited you to accompany her to the library to help her select her reading material—and perhaps something for yourself."

Mrs. Lindstrom ignored the invitation. "Are you telling me that you have no way of monitoring what books or magazines a child takes off the shelves to read?"

"Yes, that is what I'm telling you, but please realize, Mrs. Lindstrom, that all children are naturally curious, and what they can't find in the library they can always find elsewhere."

"Well, I think that's a pretty lame excuse for a tax-supported institution. I don't know what else I can do, but I imagine that for starters her father and I will have to forbid our daughter to use the library. I assume you would honor *that* instruction." And with that, Mrs. Lindstrom stormed out the door.

62

PERIODICAL CANCELLATIONS DURING TOUGH TIMES

The meeting with subject specialists and branch librarians had been a heated one, and library director Warren Hobson was not really surprised. Faced with steadily increasing periodical subscription prices over more than a decade, the Great Valley State University Library had done just about what every other major university library in the country had done—asked for more funds from the legislature and by reallocation from the university;

shifted priorities within the library, including the transfer of funds from the monographic to the serials budget; delayed staff hiring and automation; and looked, in cooperation with other nearby universities, at programs of cooperative acquisition and resource-sharing. This last step worked better in principle than in practice, Hobson realized. Not only faculty but many librarians still placed a major emphasis not on access but on outright ownership. The value system that equated quality with size of holdings was still too deeply entrenched to give way easily.

Three years ago the library had started to cut periodical titles in earnest, after already having eliminated most duplicates. The library staff was asked, in cooperation with the faculty, to identify titles that were little used, that supported programs or faculty members no longer in the institution, and that were not covered in major indexing-tools and data-base services. At first the process had not been too difficult. There were titles that could not stand the test of scrutiny, and even the faculty was agreeable as long as they felt assured that their units were not being particularly penalized. The library staff had even tackled this task with some level of enthusiasm and a great deal of ingenuity. In looking over what had been accomplished in the last three years, Hobson felt a certain amount of pleasure in the quality of his people. When the going gets tough, the tough get going, as in the old saying.

However, what had been a challenge in the first year had proved more difficult in the second and rather traumatic in the third. And now, as they faced another decision process, they had been dealt a double blow. They had just been informed by their subscription agency to expect, for reasons of dollar devaluation, inflation, and perhaps just plain greed, price increases of 12 percent for domestic and 22 percent for foreign periodicals, which led to an average of 16 percent for this internationally flavored collection, particularly in the physical sciences. In addition, the state legislature, faced simultaneously by a recession and a taxpayers' revolt, had voted the university no increase in funding whatsoever. In university budget meetings the grim news had been spelled out quite clearly. They could expect perhaps a 2 percent growth in the total budget from tuition increases of 6 percent, assuming that the increases did not cut enrollment. Faculty salaries, including those of librarians, were the institution's top priority; there was still hope that an average 4 percent salary increase, unspectacular but essential to protect against faculty raiding, could be managed for the institution as a whole. Warren felt that the library was less threatened by raiding, but he also felt strongly that librarians, already at the low end of faculty salaries, should receive at least an average 4 percent salary increase if everyone else did.

The alternatives for the university were not pleasant. They involved a decrease in staff through attrition, the replacement of high-priced retiring faculty members with lower-salaried new hires, a heavy dose of outside fundraising, and a good deal of innovation.

However, the library really had few of these options, Warren Hobson realized. Its staff, by any comparison to other ARL libraries, was already thin. Fundraising activities had brought in some money but not a great deal, and Hobson realized that giving money to the library for more materials did not have the attractiveness of other gifts. No major donor willing to supply several million dollars, perhaps in return for having the library named after him, had appeared. Fundraising efforts would of course continue and redouble, but could promise little.

When Warren had broached the library's particular problems of dealing with the continuing periodicals price increases in this environment to the university's president, she was sympathetic but not reassuring. Perhaps some reassignments within the library were possible; she suggested taking up the issue with the faculty library committee. Hobson had few expectations for the outcome of such a meeting, but he had gone through with it. A number of the members had suggested, cautiously and almost diffidently, that perhaps the library could delay some of its automation agenda, or look at ways to reduce staff, as other academic departments were doing. When Hobson pointed out that the library was already well behind its peer institutions in library automation, and resurrected the comparative staffing statistics, they fell silent; the meeting ended shortly thereafter.

It was then that the library director had appointed an internal task force of branch librarians and bibliographers to develop a plan for dealing with this budgetary crisis. That task force had just reported its failure to reach agreement on any common strategy, and the ensuing discussion had turned into bickering and accusation, with old and good friends accusing one another of unreasonableness and selfishness.

Warren had heard enough. He was not going to let the team he had nurtured so carefully be destroyed, and he therefore announced the decision on which he had been working all along, but had hoped he would not have to implement. He stood, raised his hand for silence, and then to a hushed group of librarians he announced his plan. He told them he was horrified at the bickering, and would not allow this to continue. Salary increases and librarian lines as well as other staff lines had to be protected. The university had not gotten smaller and indeed was now more complex, so pressures on the library were growing. The automation projects could not and would not be delayed, both because commitments had already been made, and because much of their future hopes for resource sharing and acquisitions decisions lay in automation. Given the staff's inability to agree, a decision he respected, he was now prepared to make an arbitrary decision. Discussions with the library budget officer had convinced him that the periodicals budget, even after all sorts of reallocations and budget tightening, could only be allowed to grow by a net of 4 percent. Based on the statistics provided by the subscription agency, this meant a base budget cut of at least 10 percent from the present budget level. The remaining 90 percent, when factored with the 16 percent price increase, would lead to a 4 percent growth.

Warren was certain that the staff could not agree that such cuts be allocated on any but an across-the-board basis, and so this is what he had decided to do. Each of the subject areas and branch libraries would be provided a printout of present titles assigned to it, together with this year's prices. Within four weeks he wanted the lists returned with cuts totaling 10 percent. Librarians were urged to consult faculty and colleagues in this process, but the responsibility was theirs. For unassigned titles the same sort of 10 percent cut would be determined by the library's central administration. Warren finished speaking, took a sip of water, and asked for reactions. There were none; they just looked at him. And so he adjourned the meeting. Hobson had not relished making this choice, but he saw no alternative.

Questions to Consider

1. The "Honor" of Being a Clerk in the Library (p. 1)

Summary: Betsy raises issues with which Francine is really already familiar but has chosen to ignore up until now. The only difference is that these problems have now been brought into the open, at least by one individual. Francine faces assessments that are both moral and political.

Questions: Should Francine simply tell Betsy that while none of this was fair, life itself is frequently unfair? If she does, what are the possible implications in her relations with Betsy, with the staff she represents, and with the community of which Betsy's family is a prominent part? If Francine does decide to open this question with municipal authorities, how should she do it? What should be her reaction if the city agrees to salary adjustments but not to additional library funding? What is the balance between fairness to the staff and service to the patrons?

Other issues: Is there any way this problem could have been avoided? What is your assessment of Francine as a manager and of the probability that she would have done anything about this issue on her own? Is it important to determine whether Betsy is speaking only for herself, or whether she has a mandate from the staff organization? Is one of the "bureaucratic" options to stall, pretending to Betsy that you are seeking solutions while really doing nothing? What do you think of the ethics of such an approach? Do such approaches work in the long term? In the short term?

2. The Enthusiastic High-Priced File Clerk (p. 3)

Summary: Ed has noted a problem, which is frankly admitted by the assistant director. Agnes, classified and paid as a cataloger, is performing the work of a file clerk, apparently with contentment and satisfaction. While the library staff certainly know about the situation, others apparently do not. The library director appears concerned about this specific issue, but even more directly about the fact that in eighteen months even the filing job will have disappeared.

Questions: Should Agnes be forced to return to her duties as a cataloger and given the opportunity for training in her revised duties? How do you assess her willingness to undertake this training and the likelihood of its success? If you pursued this course, how would you persuade her to agree? What other options are there? Changing her job description to that of a clerk, with or without a change in salary? How plausible is this in the university structure? Asking her to resign, or pressuring her to resign, or opting for some sort of early retirement? Does the university administration and/or personnel department have to be brought into this issue? Can a retirement date be firmed up or negotiated? Can another clerical job be found for her in eighteen months? How important is it that this issue be handled quietly and sensitively?

Other issues: The handling of this case up until now is a classic example of decision-avoidance. Should it have been handled directly when it first arose? How, and with what options and opportunities presented to Agnes? If you were Ed Krikorian, how would this affect your assessment of Florence Van Horne as an administrator?

3. The Reluctant New Supervisor (p. 4)

Summary: Amelia Rodriguez has been selected for promotion to the post of head of the reference department for the public library. She is considered totally qualified, but she resists accepting the offer because she does not want to be in a position of making decisions about other people's performances and futures.

Questions: Are Amelia's concerns the normal fears of a new supervisor, and should she be assured that she will do just fine? Should she be offered training and support so that she will gain confidence in her own supervisory skills? Or is the issue of her self-confidence really the basic question? Should the library accept her reasons and appoint somebody else? Should it offer her more time to think about it? Should it insist that she accept this appointment?

Other issues: Is the relationship between managers and subordinates at times as clearly a matter of management evaluation as Amelia sees it, or can different management styles mitigate the potential need to make unpleasant decisions and impart unpleasant news? Should reluctant potential managers be nevertheless urged to accept this responsibility if administration considers them qualified, or should their reluctance be accepted at face value? Does the work of Laurence Peter (the Peter principle) affect this case study? Is there a need to consider parallel career options and professional and financial growth without the necessity of accepting management responsibilities?

4. The Employee Who Wouldn't Leave (p. 6)

Summary: Harry Henderson, an excellent reference librarian, was promoted to a managerial post despite the reservations of the library director, reservations shown to have validity. Because of his perceived unsatisfactory performance in this management post, Harry was denied a further promotion. His attitude has become increasingly hostile, and while he has announced his intention to leave, he has not done so.

Questions: Can the library take action on the premise of Harry's announced resignation to secure a specific departure date? Should it do so? How should Mark Rowan react to the openly critical comments now being voiced? What is the role of Henderson's at least nominal boss, the assistant director for public services? What is a "nominal" boss? What is the role of the municipal civil service in this case? Is there a need to involve this agency?

Other issues: Harry was at one time, and presumably still is, an excellent reference librarian. What went wrong, and why? Can this situation somehow be reversed? Although this is presumably a case study about Harry, what conclusions do you draw about Mark? What, along the way, should have been the role of performance evaluation, in specific and written form?

5. Not a Member of Our Team (p. 8)

Summary: Beverly Macklin is considering several applicants for a clerical position, but is drawn to the candidacy of Shirley Walker, who is considerably older than the other clerks in the library. Peggy Riordan, a self-appointed spokesperson for the group, makes it clear that Shirley would not be an acceptable co-worker, because she would not fit into their group.

Questions: How do you balance what is clearly an age bias against the desire to have an effective working team? Would not the same situation apply for any candidate who might be "different" in terms of race, color, religion, sex, or physical disability? In her silence in response to Peggy's statement, has Beverly already weakened her case? What should she have said? What would you have said? What would you do now? Call Peggy back, hire Shirley anyway but say nothing, select another candidate? What does Peggy expect?

Other issues: Is there a need for sensitivity training, or at least an open and frank discussion perhaps involving affirmative action staff, for this library? Can you assume from this that Peggy, and perhaps the staff at large, is simply bigoted? Assuming that you undertake some sort of sensitivity training, how do you present and implement it?

6. Concern about Radiation (p. 10)

Summary: The public library is planning to automate, with funds provided by outside sources. Teri, who is scheduled to work on the computer terminals, tells the library director that she is concerned about the possible effect of such an assignment on her ability to have children. She acknowledges that there is no scientific certainty in support of her fears; nevertheless, she wants to be transferred to a job that doesn't involve computers.

Questions: What are the legal issues in this case? Would discussion with the library's attorney or with the appropriate municipal officers be appropriate? Assuming that there is no legal basis for her complaint, since many individuals now work with terminals routinely, do you offer her a transfer if you have a noncomputer position available? If you do, what is the possibility that you are establishing a precedent you might not be able to handle? If you do it for Teri, do you have to do it for everyone? If the library is unable or unwilling to accommodate to her request, what are the options? Do they include transfer to another agency? If there is no such position, do you ask her to resign? Do you fire her? If so, should it be now or when the computers arrive?

Other issues: This is an emotional issue. What is the possible role of education and counseling, not only for Teri but also for other employees? What is the concern that Teri's attitude may evoke sympathy for her from the rest of the staff and the general public? What is the concern about a ripple effect of panic? Could this discussion between Teri and Minna have been anticipated and avoided?

7. A Circulation Clerk Gone Sour (p. 11)

Summary: A longtime clerical employee in the corporate technical information center has an excellent performance history, but over the last nine months both her performance and her attendance have suffered. There are rumors about the employee's relationship with her husband, but these are neither acknowledged nor substantiated. The supervisor makes an effort to discuss the issue in a friendly conversation after a performance evaluation in which the employee is rated merely as satisfactory; however, she is rebuffed.

Questions: Should the supervisor discuss this issue with higher management and the personnel department? Is there at present any basis for conjecture? For disciplinary action? Given the situation as described, was the rating of "satisfactory" accurate or generous? Do we concentrate on helping Agnes through whatever problem she may be having, or do we concentrate on job performance? Should we try for some combination of the two approaches?

Other issues: Has Sandra's action up until now been correct? Has it been too fast, too slow, too blunt, too wishy-washy? How do you reach an employee who does not want to be reached? Is this a potential appeal for "tough love"?

8. The Disappearing Printer (p. 14)

Summary: The library director, who knows little about printing matters, hires a replacement printer primarily on the recommendation of the printer who is leaving. The new printer fails to appear on schedule, after having first asked for extra time to complete work for a former employer, and leaves no message. The former employer denies that there was any delay in the transfer. When he was missing for three days, after the rescheduled start date, the printer's wife calls to explain a family emergency, but says her husband will start on Monday.

Questions: Do you consider acceptable the explanation for his failure to appear? What about the discrepancy between the claim that he required extra days to finish an earlier assignment and the former employer's refutation of this? Are you disturbed that all the calls come from Mrs. Morton? Do you really even know who called? Do you let Morton start on Monday (assuming he shows up)? Do you cancel his employment? Do you have the right to do this? Do you want to talk to Morton before Monday? To determine what?

Other issues: Was this situation properly or badly handled? If the latter, what should have been done? Would you now have concerns about the reliability of this printer? To what extent are such conjectures appropriate or fair? Does the fact that Morton is not yet an employee (as opposed to the previous case) make a difference?

9. The Arrest of a Maintenance Employee (p. 16)

Summary: The library director learns from her Sunday paper that a library maintenance employee was arrested Saturday night, and attempts to learn about the case from the police department that afternoon. The next day, after she has received a positive report on the employee's performance record from his supervisor but before she has a chance to talk to him, she is brought a note of resignation, written on the assumption that he would be fired in any case.

Questions: Can you fault Eileen McDougall's actions up to now? Should she have done anything else, or done anything sooner? Should she now simply accept the resignation and consider the case closed? Should she assure Hamilton that there is no need to resign, at least until after the disposition of the case? If he accepts that offer, do you put him back to work? Do you suspend him? If so, with or without pay? What, if anything, do you need to say to the library staff? To the library board? How would you anticipate reactions from this conservative community?

Other issues: Hamilton is legally innocent until found guilty, but how does this balance against the library's public image? Assuming he is guilty or pleads guilty, how does that affect his work status? Should library maintenance workers be held to a higher standard of conduct? Was the newspaper article fair?

10. Tell Me a Story (p. 18)

Summary: Upon taking a new job as director of a small public library, Anita decides that Marie, who has been the children's librarian for a considerable period, has a strong interest in children's literature but very little interest in children.

Questions: Can Anita be certain of her diagnosis? How can she find out whether her assumptions are valid? To whom does she speak about her concerns? Marie? The library board? Does she just let the matter go? Is there a way to weave more specific expectations into the job description and performance evaluations? Anita did not hire Marie, and we are not told who did, but Anita is new. What does that suggest in the way of strategies? Is the solution more dangerous than the problem?

Other issues: How likely is the possibility of a children's librarian who likes children's literature but not children? Can Marie's attitude be changed, and what are the alternatives if it isn't? Does the presence of supportive staff people and the fact that nobody has been complaining make a difference? How should hiring and interview procedures forestall such a possibility as this?

11. A Conflict of Value Systems (p. 20)

Summary: Donna, the public library's assistant director for public services, suffers a tragic loss through the death of her teenage daughter at the hands of a drunk driver. She returns to work with a changed value system, giving first priority to her increasing public work to combat drunk driving. The library director is concerned that this shift in emphasis is affecting her work in the library, but his efforts to discuss this matter with Donna are disastrously rebuffed.

Questions: Did Jim prepare badly for this meeting with Donna? Should he first have talked to the library board? To Donna's husband? Should he have handled the interview differently? Should he have understood that in her frame of mind Donna was in no mood to worry about library issues? What should Jim do now? Accept the situation as it is, recognizing that it might get worse? Remove Donna from supervisory responsibilities? Dock her for her absences? Suggest that she take a leave of absence, or a part-time job? Fire her? Accept the situation as it is and make the best of it?

Other issues: Donna is an individual of considerable prominence, who can also draw on a great deal of public sympathy. What are the risks in any corrective action that Jim might take? Should he leave well enough alone, and simply "contribute" Donna's time, scheduling around her? Does he need library board and municipal concurrence for this? Is this problem temporary, and is time on Jim's side?

12. I before E Except after C (p. 23)

Summary: Library director Hastings discovers that a minority employee, hired with university financial support to overcome clerical backlogs, has very little work to do, and learns from his staff that they are giving her very little dictaphone work because she is a poor speller. They have not told him because they like the employee and are afraid he will fire her.

Questions: Is the staff's conspiracy of silence an acceptable approach? Is Hastings justified in his anger? Are there other options available, including additional education and/or training, the implementation of spell-checker programs, or one-on-one counseling and explanation of errors? Should

Donna be fired? Transferred to another position for which spelling accuracy is not as critical? If so, how should this be handled in discussions with her? With the university personnel department?

Other issues: Could this problem have been avoided through more stringent testing of potential candidates? If so, what should you do if no better-qualified candidate appears? What is the sensitivity in taking action at this point, given the university's commitment and funding support? Is Donna really aware of her shortcomings, or is she in the dark about why she is receiving so few assignments? If the latter, is this an act of kindness or unfairness?

13. Withholding of Interlibrary Loans (p. 26)

Summary: The state university library administration discovers by accident that the librarian responsible for interlibrary loans has been withholding service to countries she considers in violation of human rights. When confronted with this discovery, she acknowledges her action but notes that supplying these services would violate both her conscience and resolutions taken by the American Library Association.

Questions: Can the moral issue here be separated from management responsibility? Does Susan have the right to do unilaterally what she is doing? Is the library director wise in seeking to avoid a public confrontation? If so, how can he best avoid this? By looking the other way while Susan continues to act on these principles? By telling her to transfer "offensive" requests to another librarian? Would this satisfy her? Should he transfer her? Should he give her an ultimatum? Should university administration be consulted, or do you think they would rather the director handle this problem himself?

Other issues: What should an individual do who finds parts of job assignments contrary to personal convictions? Is this an appropriate topic for a staff discussion and perhaps a staff decision? What is the impact of the vote by the ALA council?

14. Free Searching for the Poor (p. 27)

Summary: The library director discovers that a reference librarian, charged with the responsibility of implementing library board policy of charging for on-line searches, acknowledges that he has been waiving the fee for those he feels are unable to pay. Rather than apologize and promise to mend his ways, he notes that he finds the payment policy offensive and contrary to principles of librarianship in which he fervently believes. Unless he is allowed to continue waiving the fee for these people, he may find it impossible to stay at the library.

Questions: Did Sybil make an appropriate agreement with the board, or should she have done something else? How well did she handle the discussion with Jeff? Was it all right for her to confide that she disliked her own policy, and hoped to change it in the future? How valid are Jeff's criteria for determining ability to pay? Are other criteria possible to determine who can afford to pay? What of Jeff's point that this library policy violates professional ethical standards? What are Sybil's present options? Should she allow Jeff to continue, now that she knows? Ask the board what to do? Encourage Jeff to change his mind, or find some compromise under which perhaps somebody else would make the determination of ability to pay? Allow Jeff to quit?

Other issues: Like the preceding case study (and many situations in libraries), professional responsibilities as assigned can come into conflict with personal commitment. What should be done when this occurs? Would it be better to eliminate on-line searching entirely rather than charge for it? Would this help the people unable to pay? Would it make one feel better?

15. The Use of a Parking Space (p. 29)

Summary: The library director learns from a committee of secretaries that his own secretary, not liked by the others, is using his reserved parking space when she knows that he will not be using it. They feel it should be available on a rotating basis so the convenience of it is available equally to everyone.

Questions: Is this a trivial and petty issue, and should Bernie simply tell the other secretaries not to be so childish? Is this a serious or a frivolous problem? Would the problem be different if the secretary were well liked, and the director had found out only by accident? Should Bernie now acknowledge to the secretaries in his office that he did not know, or should he pretend that he had given his approval? Should he insist that his space remain vacant in his absence? Should he try to develop some sort of rotating policy when he is away? Is it worth the trouble? Would it be preferable to eliminate all assigned parking spaces? If he tells Shirley not to use his parking space in the future, how does he explain how he discovered she was using the space?

Other issues: Sometimes issues not particularly substantive for the operation of the library can cause a great deal of unrest if there is a perception of unfairness or favoritism. It can be argued that the issue is important even if for no other reason than that a group of employees think it is important. The director can, of course, shift the blame to Shirley by pointing out that if she made more of an attempt to be collegial with the other secretaries this would not have happened. Is this a good idea?

16. A Conflict of Interest? (p. 31)

Summary: Jill Monroe is a recent employee at the university library and the director is very pleased with her work. She has responsibility for the selection of subscription agents and has switched the library account to a new vendor that appears to be performing satisfactorily. The library director receives an anonymous letter charging Jill with a personal relationship with the president of the new vendor, and thus with a conflict of interest.

Questions: Should anonymous letters simply be thrown away? Should Tom try to determine whether or not a personal relationship does exist? If so, how? By asking Jill? How would such a conversation be broached? Should he review the documentation concerning the choice of vendors to see if any irregularity exists? Should he talk to anyone else in the university about this?

Other issues: Is the appearance of favoritism a problem whether it actually exists? Does it matter whether the president of Communico is single? Should Tom remove Jill from the selection process for the next contract? If so, how does he explain this to her? Could this issue have been avoided? Does the university (or the library) have a policy that addresses issues such as this?

17. Just Work; Don't Ask So Many Questions! (p. 32)

Summary: A recent graduate calls her library school dean to ask his advice about a problem. A university library cataloger, she finds that her supervisor is not an individual whom she can respect, because some of the supervisor's policies don't seem to make sense. Her supervisor has just told her not to raise so many issues, but simply to follow the policies as stated. The dean does not know the supervisor, but does know the director of the library.

Questions: Sheila is asking Emory Woolcott for advice. Should he offer specific suggestions, or just general sympathy? If the former, can he be certain he fully understands all the ramifications without talking to Adelaide, her supervisor? Should he offer to do that? If he gives her specific advice, what would it be? Look for another job? Continue to raise questions? Try to talk to her supervisor again? Talk to the library director about the problem? Should *he* offer to talk to the library director? And should he do so without telling Sheila?

Other issues: Could this problem have been avoided through a more careful job search or through better interviewing procedures? Is Henrietta, the library director, aware of this issue? Is she satisfied with the way the cataloging department is functioning? Is there any indication that other catalogers feel as Sheila does? Is it important to find out? Who would be supposed to do this? Should Sheila ask for a transfer to another department, even though she wants to be a cataloger? Would this strategy be preferable to seeking to leave after such a short time? If she leaves, should Sheila tell Henrietta (or Adelaide) the reason at that time?

18. Fear of Flying (p. 34)

Summary: The dean of libraries of a western university wants to appoint the associate dean to an important LC committee. He declines the appointment, stating that he has an aversion to flying caused by the death of his father in a plane crash.

Questions: Should Ingeborg simply accept Frank's answer sympathetically, or should she urge him to seek psychological counseling? Should she demand that he do so? Should she ask him to recommend another staff member for the appointment? Should she simply decline to participate? If so, what does she tell LC? Assuming that refusing to fly will hurt Frank's professional career, does Ingeborg make a special effort to persuade him to seek help for his own sake? Does the fact that he is a minority staff member make a difference?

Other issues: Is there a university policy Ingeborg should consult, or university officials she should contact? If so, does this breach Frank's right to privacy of his feelings? Could she just tell him to go by train even though it obviously would add a lot of time to the trip? Is this an acceptable solution for the library, assuming that Frank agrees? Ingeborg must be careful not to make snap statements about a delicate area in which she has neither expertise nor training.

19. Bypassed for Promotion (p. 36)

Summary: Cataloger Deborah Higdon has not received a promotion she confidently expected because of her seniority—instead it has gone to someone else. Now she complains about this to the university library's associate dean for administration and personnel, Marianne Hoogedorn. She states that her supervisor, Francis Schimmel, has told her she did not receive the promotion because of a lack of professional activities and leadership skills, but she adds that these requirements had never been mentioned to her.

Questions: Is it disturbing that the personnel department appears so unaware of the procedures under which this promotion was made? Can Marianne draw any conclusion without talking to Frances Schimmel? Should she ask Deborah's agreement before she does this? Are there other individuals to whom she needs to talk? The library director? The appointment has already been made; therefore, what does one now say to Deborah? Apologize? Urge her to prepare herself for the next promotion? What are the mechanisms for developing better communication skills and leadership? Does one talk tough to her, and tell her she was naive to assume so much?

Other issues: There is no mention of a job description for either Deborah's job or the new one. Nor is there any reference to performance evaluations, which should concentrate not only on the past but on opportunities for the future. What does this suggest about the library and its assistant director, let alone the head of cataloging? Is there a larger problem here than the immediate concern of Deborah Higdon?

20. An Allocation of Merit Increases (p. 38)

Summary: Fred has decided to give Marybeth a smaller-than-average salary increase, in part to release funds for larger increases for employees he considers more deserving, and in part to send a message of his lack of total satisfaction with her job performance. Before he can act, Marybeth states that she expects a more-than-average salary increase, and that she will file a grievance if she doesn't receive it.

Questions: What does this case study suggest about the adequacy of present performance-evaluation policies? Is a smaller salary increase a good way to "send a message" if there has been no prior statement of dissatisfaction? Assuming that Fred's assessment of subordinate performance is valid (although there is no way of knowing this), is this approach fair? Can it be defended? How should he answer Marybeth? Should he tell her what he plans to do? Should he revise his planned actions? Should he talk to his boss? To the personnel department?

Other issues: This case study is written specifically from the viewpoint of the supervisor; without some validation or documentation we have no way of knowing whether his assessment is valid—and more to the point, neither will the individuals who receive Marybeth's grievance complaint. Fred's assessments may be accurate, but how valid are they if neither the positives nor the negatives have been documented? Is he well prepared for the fight that Marybeth offers him? If not, should he modify the salary increase percentages? Given the fixed total of dollars available, how fair is this now to Anna and Terri? What does all of this suggest about the abilities of Fred Plunkett? About the personnel policies of the corporation?

21. Let's Give Her a Try; It May Work Out (p. 40)

Summary: The library, which is looking for a junior clerk, is sent an interviewee (Suzanne) who does not seem to meet the job description and who is not particularly interested in the post. Discussion with university personnel reveals that she is about to be fired by the purchasing department, but has charged sexual harassment and threatened to sue. A transfer to the library, where administrators are all female, is seen as an opportunity to blunt the harassment charge. The library is assured that if the employee doesn't work out, she can be terminated.

Questions: How strongly can one assume that personnel will back the library if the candidate is still found to be "sloppy, inattentive, and rude"? Doesn't President Graubart still lurk in the background, in his desire to avoid legal complications? Should the library try to be a good "team player," or should it insist on an employee who meets its requirements? Should the purchasing department be contacted for further validation of Suzanne's performance? While sexual harassment presumably is not a possibility in the library, might there be other potential grounds for a suit? Should the library give Suzanne the chance because she might be telling the truth?

Other issues: Can it be assumed that the library was chosen because of its all-female administrative staff, or perhaps because it is considered that the quality of employee performance there is not as important? Are there risks in either perception for the library? Which risks are more appropriate to take? If Suzanne meets the job description, can the library still reject her?

22. Go, Team, Go (p. 41)

Summary: An undergraduate student working in the library has been putting little notes concerning football rivalries into interlibrary loan shipments. When the library director finds out from a recipient he tells the student to stop, and the student agrees. However, the university president, alerted by another recipient, demands to know the name of the student so that disciplinary action can be taken.

Questions: Is this an issue of principle for librarian Huckaby that is worth fighting over? Should he tell the president that he has given his word to the student not to identify him, though that's not really true? Should he try to reason with or dissuade the president? Should he give in to the president's request for the student's name, and then try to dissuade the dean of students from doing anything serious to the student? Would offering to dismiss the student from his job be an appropriate compromise?

Other issues: It is well to remember that even a seemingly trivial incident can become important—even reaching a crisis. Did the librarian handle the case badly in not taking it as seriously as the president now takes it? Should he have done something else with regard to the student? Given President Grubble's attitude, is it likely that the dean of students will protect the student from expulsion? Is all of this worth fighting about when the relationship between the library and the university president may be at stake?

23. Please Don't Let My Marriage Be Destroyed! (p. 43)

Summary: The husband of a printing department employee writes a confidential letter to the library director stating that his wife is having an affair with her supervisor, that she wanted to break it off but had been unable to. He asks that the two be separated from daily contact.

Questions: Is this a personal matter involving consenting adults and not the library's business at all? If so, how do you respond to Harrison? By telephone, face-to-face meeting, or letter? Is there concern that Mrs. Harrison may want to break off the affair as her husband suggests, but "does not have the strength to do so"? Is there an issue of possible sexual harassment here? Should the director talk to Mrs. Harrison? Alone or with her husband? Should he talk to Warren Brinson? Should he tell Harrison that if his wife has anything to say she should come to see him herself? If you pursue this question, under what grounds might you fire either or both employees? Is transferring Mrs. Harrison a viable option? Suppose she suggests it?

Other issues: This is a delicate problem. On the one hand, there is no basis for assessing the validity of Mr. Harrison's charges. On the other hand, if there is an issue of coercion and harassment here, with Mrs. Harrison afraid to say anything, it becomes another problem; you can be criticized later for having ignored the letter. Could this situation have been avoided? Should this communication be kept in confidence, or should perhaps the university attorney be consulted?

24. The Drinking Employee (p. 44)

Summary: The library director discovers that an employee has been chronically absent, presumably because of a drinking problem, over the last four months. Both the employee's staff and her supervisors have been covering for her absence because they feel sorry for her and hope the situation will improve.

Questions: If Beulah has a drinking problem, is this a good way to deal with it? If not, what would be more supportive? What about Jankowski's and Watanabe's response? Does it represent an act of loyalty? A pointless gesture that avoids the real problem? A serious breach of library policy and management responsibility worthy of disciplinary action? What sort of action? What of Beulah's subordinates and all the others who knew and kept silent? What should be done about Beulah now? Should someone talk to her? Should Watanabe or Jankowski be told to talk to her? Is there a role for Marlys here? For other departments in the university? Has it been absolutely established that she is drinking? Why she is drinking? Does one offer her support? Demand proper attention to her job and treatment for her problem, or the alternative of disciplinary action? A combination of the two?

Other issues: Alcoholism, if indeed this is a case of alcoholism, is a disease, not a crime subject to punishment. At the same time, it is up to the employee to undertake or agree to necessary actions to restore her satisfactory performance. How should Marlys, who is personnel officer but failed to know what seemed to be common knowledge, be assessed? Is this her fault?

25. Vehicle Safety and Individual Rights (p. 45)

Summary: A prominent library user notes that the library's praiseworthy campaign to support traffic safety is undermined by the fact that one of the children's librarians drives a motorcycle without wearing a helmet. The librarian counters by saying that this is his personal preference, and that in this jurisdiction wearing helmets is not required by law.

Questions: Is Jeff correct in stating that this is his own business, that the patron complaining about him should mind hers? If the matter with Jeff is dropped, what do you tell Mrs. Overmeyer? Do you try to persuade Jeff to wear a helmet? If so, for his sake? For the sake of the library's image? What are the risks for the library in Mrs. Overmeyer's displeasure?

Other issues: Could this have been avoided? What sort of damage control if any do you consider appropriate, or are the library's campaign (in which Jeff may not be participating) and his own safety habits unrelated? How would you respond if the allegation were sexual promiscuity? Smoking where children can see him? Does the fact that he is a children's librarian as opposed to an adult services librarian make a difference?

26. A Potential Conflict of Viewpoints—1 (p. 47)

Summary: Head of reference Francine Thayer and reference librarian Toni Dvorak are about to have their regular annual performance evaluation, but they bring very different concerns to the discussion. Francine is concerned that Toni is not making adequate progress along the tenure track; Toni is concerned that a lack of adequate staffing and funding combined with her own personal problems in being the sole caretaker for her mother make both the evaluation process and any expectation of professional participation something of a joke.

Questions: Is this the right time for Francine to raise her concerns, or has she perhaps waited too long? What sort of reinforcement is she prepared to offer, and to what extent does she anticipate Toni's reaction? Have the reasons for Toni's average (and smaller than some) salary increases been openly discussed as part of the evaluation process? How would you assess the quality of that communication process? How do you assess Toni's concern that the staff is overworked and that professional participation support funds are not available as part of this process? To what extent is Toni's family responsibility relevant to this discussion? How does Francine deal with this issue, assuming that Toni brings it up? How adequate do you consider the evaluation communication process in this library?

Other issues: Differences in viewpoint and in emphasis characterize the performance evaluation process. To what extent do supervisors need to prepare themselves for that reality? Some supervisors are notoriously reluctant to communicate bad news or criticism. Do you see any of this tendency in Francine?

27. A Potential Conflict of Viewpoints—2 (p. 49)

Summary: Cataloging department head Marie Schultz is leaving, and considers cataloger Debbie Grimsley the best qualified to replace her. At this meeting Marie plans to offer Debbie this promotion, and she is pleased at the prospect. Debbie approaches the performance evaluation as routine. She particularly values the freedom and flexibility that her present job gives her.

Questions: Does the fact that Debbie is the best cataloger and well liked make her automatically the best candidate for promotion? How well does Marie really understand Debbie and her value system? What does this suggest about the communication process that exists in this library? Are there options for Debbie outside the management promotion process? How encouraging and supportive should Marie be, and to what extent should she urge or pressure Debbie to accept? If Debbie turns down the promotion, what is Marie's next step? What does it mean for Debbie's future in the library? Should Debbie have been offered the position? Should she accept?

Other issues: Like the preceding case study, this one suggests a lack of in-depth communication, since Marie has never determined what Debbie's value system is. Has any real harm been done up to this point? Is there potential for serious harm if this case is now mishandled? How could all of this have been avoided?

28. The Children's Room for Staff Babysitting (p. 51)

Summary: The head of the children's department tells the library director that the director's secretary has been bringing her children to the library for care on an emergency basis about once a month, starting about six months ago; she feels that this is inappropriate, and the library cannot handle this responsibility. The library director has been completely unaware of this process. Both the head of the children's department and the secretary are black; the director suspects that this may be a factor in Nancy's decision to ask for Nicole's help.

Questions: Has Nicole waited too long to bring this problem to Frank's attention? Should she have turned Nancy down the second time she asked, and suggested that Nancy talk to Frank? In accepting a "rather expensive" gift, has Nicole already compromised her position? Is Nicole reacting defensively because both she and Nancy are black, and is this an issue? Should Nancy have told Frank about the problem? What would Frank have said? What should Frank do now? Tell Nicole to refuse? Tell Nancy not to ask Nicole for such help? How can he do this without implicating Nicole?

Other issues: Whereas this issue is specific, the problems may be generic. Does the library need a formalized policy concerning the care of children with its walls? Employees' children, patrons' children, or both? Should the library have an appropriate child care facility? Is this an issue that Frank should bring to the board? To the municipal administration? Should there be a library policy covering such issues? What of Frank's sense that this was acceptable as an emergency the first time but perhaps not the second time? Actually Frank has said nothing substantive. What do you think he will say next? Are there potential legal issues here with regard to the library's suitability as a child care facility?

29. A Request for Transfer (p. 53)

Summary: Becky Bartram expresses an interest in the open position of genealogy librarian, and assumes that she will receive this transfer. Personnel director Sharon McCorkle, who is not aware of Becky's specific academic qualifications but considers her unsuited for this position from a personality standpoint, has already decided that Becky cannot have this transfer.

Questions: Does Sharon by herself have the right to reach such a finite decision of unsuitability? If personality factors are important in the job description for genealogy librarian, should they be in the job description? How likely is it that the job description includes this information? Should Becky's perceived personality shortcomings have been mentioned to her in earlier performance reviews? Or, since they did not interfere with her performance in the job of cataloger, would this have been unnecessarily cruel? Should Becky simply be told not to bother to apply? What do you anticipate as her reaction? Should some excuse be found instead for not appointing her?

Other issues: What does this case study tell you about the performance evaluation procedures in effect in this library? Would it be fair to expect Sharon to know more about Becky's academic qualifications and interests? Totally outside this case study are the two supervisors involved, Becky's present supervisor and the supervisor for the genealogy librarian. How important is it that they be consulted? Does Sharon do this now or wait for the formal application from Becky?

30. Intellectual Moonlighting on Library Time? (p. 54)

Summary: The library director receives, anonymously, a book review that reports on a book that he believes was almost certainly written by a library staff member. That individual had never mentioned such a book. The library director now suspects that the librarian was spending much of his time on this book when he should have been working on library problems.

Questions: Does Wilfred need to be careful not to jump to conclusions? Is this author the same Roger Parrish? How would he find out? If it is, has Parrish done anything wrong? Is there evidence that he has neglected his library work? If this is the same person can Wilfred be certain this has deliberately been kept a secret? Should he ignore the news clipping? Should he ask his "nominal" supervisor? What does the designation *nominal supervisor* mean? Should Wilfred confront Parrish directly? Should he "snoop around"? If Parrish is asked directly and confirms it, should Wilfred's attitude be accusative or congratulatory?

Other issues: Are there any sort of job descriptions or expectations against which to measure Parrish's performance? Does the fact that he was "almost never in the office" when Wilfred called mean anything specific? Should there be any sort of assessment of Parrish from the scholars and faculty members with whom he is presumably working? This case provides an opportunity to jump to conclusions and to overreact, both very dangerous management tendencies. The supervisor could end up looking quite stupid.

31. A Concern about Possible Nepotism (p. 55)

Summary: The library director has a report from the search committee that forwards two names for the post of assistant director for technical services. One is a highly qualified outside candidate, the other an internal candidate who also is considered the sentimental choice of the staff and the director. If the internal candidate is appointed, then her daughter will be working for her in a direct line of supervision.

Questions: Is the issue of possible nepotism the primary question, or is it the secondary question as to who should be hired? In either case, do you have any fault to find with the search process procedures? Is Amanda's feeling that she is expected to appoint Sue Haddock realistic? Given the fact that she is indecisive about it, is this a good reason to appoint the internal candidate? The external candidate? If she selects Sue, what does she do about her daughter? Leave her where she is? Transfer her to public services? Ask her to resign? Ask university administration for a policy ruling? Is this complication a good reason for appointing Eastbrook?

Other issues: What is your assessment of Byrd as a decision-oriented director? Would a referral to a strong and specific job description help? What of the potential for a candidate's future growth and development? Can one operate on the basis of "plausible" decisions, or is something firmer needed in order to decide? How does one get something firmer? Could this potential problem have been anticipated? Avoided?

32. An AIDS Case on the Library Staff (p. 57)

Summary: An assistant children's librarian at a rural county library announces to the library director that she has the AIDS virus. She also asks that the director mention this situation to no one else.

Questions: Do you agree with what Celeste has said to Cindy? How would you have handled this initial discussion, considering that you would have had no early preparation for it? What are Celeste's responsibilities for informing anyone else—Cindy's supervisor, the library board, the county government, other library employees, patrons? If you feel that she has such responsibilities, when should she do this? Is it an option to move Cindy to another position in which she won't have direct contact with others, particularly children? Suppose Cindy disagrees with such an approach?

Other issues: What sort of community reaction is it realistic to expect and how would you handle it? Ultimately, and insofar as you are a free agent unfettered by county policy or board action, what is the extent of your responsibility to Cindy and to others? What is the role of the ALA statements of principle in this case study?

33. The Community Room (p. 59)

Summary: Library policies for the use of the library's community room allow a group of young people whom some consider satanists to use the room. The chairman of the board, who has always been on excellent terms with the library director, asks the director to draft revised policies that would exclude groups such as this and convenes a board meeting to approve these changes. At the meeting, the library director reports instead that he has decided to recommend no changes, in the belief that this represents a dangerous trend toward censorship. The chairman of the board, angry at this report, adjourns the meeting.

Questions: Are ALA policies here binding or advisory? Are there legal issues for which an opinion should be sought from the city attorney's office? Do you agree with Peter Campanis's stand on the issue of intellectual freedom? If Lyle Pocklington and the board simply draw their own policy, is Peter then left with a hollow victory? Has he jeopardized his job? Is this really a case of censorship, or do you agree with Lyle that this is not such a concern? How did Peter handle his interaction with Lyle? Was it wise simply to spring this decision on him at the board meeting, or should he have done something else? What happens next?

Other issues: It should be clear that this case study consists of two quite separate issues. The first concerns the substance of library policy for the use of the community room and the proposed change in that policy designed specifically to eliminate its use by one group. The second involves the communication relationship between Peter Campanis and Lyle Pocklington, a relationship that has prospered up to this point but is now in grave danger.

34. The High and Hidden Cost of Cooperation (p. 61)

Summary: Librarian Polly Morton has determined that the cooperative interlibrary loan network is costing her college library, and therefore her college, a considerable amount of money. This is because state subsidies do not cover what she considers to be the real costs; and also, because her library's service being so much better than that of the state university's, other libraries borrow from it to a disproportionate degree.

Questions: Should Polly tell the college president what she has determined? What are the risks of doing this? What are the risks of not doing this? Should she make some sort of recommendation to the president if she tells him? If so, what? Should she simply tell her staff to decrease the quality of the service to that of the level of the state university? Should she appeal to the state for an increase in subsidy? Threaten the state if she does not receive it?

Other issues: Does this situation represent a conflict between management responsibilities and responsibilities to the profession or to society at large? If so, are such potential conflicts likely to increase as managers are expected to become more fiscally responsible?

35. My Niece Needs a Job (p. 63)

Summary: Library trustee Harry Eberstadt alerts public library director James Bryant to the fact that his niece would be applying for a public library professional position. While Eberstadt makes no overt demand that his niece be hired, Bryant finds his manner intrusive and annoying. He realizes that, without even knowing anything about the candidate, he doesn't want to hire her.

Questions: Did Bryant handle the conversation with Eberstadt well or badly? How would you have handled it? Does Bryant have a valid concern in feeling that he cannot now consider Amy Carlson as a regular candidate? Should he take pains to make sure she gets hired, if qualified, in order to placate Eberstadt? Should he make sure she doesn't get hired in order to send Eberstadt a message? How fair is this to Amy? Assuming that in her application Amy does not mention her relationship to a trustee, should he make sure not to tell the rest of the staff, and perhaps let somebody else make the hiring decision? Suppose she does mention it? Is there an issue of nepotism here?

Other issues: The issue can cause difficulties, surprisingly, either if Amy is an excellent candidate or if she is not. If she *is* well qualified and is hired, will there be suspicion? If she is not hired because of her relationship to Harry Eberstadt, is this fair? Do you also see the mirror image of this problem if she is *not* a particularly impressive candidate? Would the existence of some sort of policy help? Would such a policy include uncles and nieces, among other relationships?

36. Public and Corporate Ethics (p. 64)

Summary: Special librarian Connie, using the corporate offices copy machine because hers requires repair, inadvertently finds a memorandum from a vice-president to the president that suggests a strategy for real estate development that she considers totally unethical. She is angry, and considers sending this memorandum to the media anonymously.

Questions: Connie has several options. She can destroy the memorandum or simply return it to the office copier; she can send anonymous copies to the media, or send copies to the media and sign her name; or she can confront President Hayes and ask him what he is going to do about this. Can you think of any other options? What do you think of the options presented? Does Connie know how Hayes will react to this recommendation and whether this will really be the corporate strategy? Should she wait to find out and then perhaps act? Should she quit her job rather than work for such an organization? If she does act, is she going to get the corporate secretaries into trouble for letting her use the copier?

Other issues: Loyalty to the employer who pays one's salary, and keeping faith with one's own principles, can sometimes cause a dilemma for any employee. Is this such a case? If President Hayes or Vice-President Lee had personally asked her to do something that she considered unethical or immoral, would that make a difference? What should she do then?

37. A Case of De Facto Self-Segregation (p. 66)

Summary: Reacting to a concern raised by a black library trustee, director Elizabeth Moberley has undertaken a conscious plan of mandated transfers to assure that white and black librarians do not work exclusively in areas in which they serve patrons of the same race. She expects and receives some opposition to these transfers from white staff members, but to her surprise also from black staff members and even black patrons.

Questions: Was this policy change introduced too hastily, without adequate communication with the staff and the community? Are the objections of staff members who prefer the convenience of working closer to home valid? Are the objections of minority staff members who prefer to serve as role models valid? What should Elizabeth do now? Enforce the policy on the assumption that people will get used to it? Return to the board with her findings? Speak directly to Reverend Washington, since some of the objecting parents might be his own parishioners? Since there are more white staff members, would it be a valid policy to disperse these while continuing to allow black staff members to select their preferred areas of work?

Other issues: Is there a potential conflict between the desire to end all vestiges of segregation and the desire to provide role models within the community? If so, how should the library deal with this? Is such a concern an appropriate issue for the public library in any case, or should the library concentrate on quality of service for all constituencies, as well as on minority recruitment?

38. Pick a Branch Library to Close (p. 68)

Summary: Newly elected mayor Oliver Crafton promises Brookton an administration based on budget cutting, austerity, and tough decisions. His meeting with Library director Barbara Hanover is gentler than most. He avows his support for the library, but argues that a gesture must be made. He suggests a study to identify and close the branch least productive in terms of cost and usage. Barbara already knows that this will be the Martin Luther King branch.

Questions: How essential is the immediate rapport developed between the mayor and librarian? He has offered her an olive branch; should she seize it or should she fight him? Should she agree to close a branch but suggest other criteria for determining which one? Would this be acceptable to Crafton? How dangerous is such an action if the residents of the area selected decide that the process was rigged? If she fights Crafton, how should she do it? And with what hope of success? Is half a loaf better than none? Is there a possibility of court intervention if the branch specifically developed to serve the black community is closed? Crafton never mentioned a specific branch; should Barbara point out this risk to him? Privately or publicly? Are there other options she could suggest that meet his criteria for the appearance of economy without closing branches?

Other issues: Assuming that a branch must be closed, is it appropriate to determine "effectiveness" through a process of comparing cost and service activity? If not, how would you approach the process of rank ordering?

39. Rejection of a Tax Appeal (p. 71)

Summary: Despite the presumed strong support of the mayor, the library's appeal for an increase in the tax base has been rejected and cannot be resurrected for at least one year. Library director Margaret Rutkowski knows that programs have been started for which there is no adequate funding. She is beginning to prepare an analysis of service curtailments that must be made when she receives a phone call from the mayor's administrative assistant. The mayor will be unavailable for several days and plans to talk to Margaret in about a month. However, he wants her to call an immediate news conference to reassure the citizens that library service quality will not decline despite the denial of the tax request.

Questions: Should Margaret refuse to make any public statement without first talking to the mayor? What are the risks for her in this? If she does make a public statement, what should she say? Should she reassure everyone, should she make a generally optimistic but nonspecific statement, or should she suggest that things will indeed now get worse? Was she wrong to have started new services without the assurance of funding? Are there any political initiatives she can take before the mayor returns, such as discussions with the board, the Friends of the Library, newspaper editors, or the chamber of commerce? How can she determine the depth of the mayor's commitment to library services?

Other issues: There are risks in confronting the mayor, there are risks in not confronting him. How can Margaret assess the balance of those risks? Can you suggest a better strategy for hedging her bets and for dealing with the mayor? What, if anything, with the benefit of hindsight, do you now feel she should have done differently?

40. The Gift of a White Elephant (p. 75)

Summary: The university president, while agreeing privately that the Hazeltyne collection probably doesn't warrant housing as a separate entity in the university library, argues that this is necessary to please the donor and to secure other donations from him. He notes that the library has room, and that he will supply any funds necessary to make this happen. Library director Joanna Miller argues that giving this collection separate status would be a waste of space and make the university a laughing stock.

Questions: On what issues do President Shoemaker and library director Miller agree with regard to this collection, and on what issues do they disagree? How would you evaluate the communication exchange taking place between the two? Is either (or perhaps both) of these people being unreasonable? Since Shoemaker has already accepted the gift on behalf of the university, what are Miller's realistic options? Might this be a good opportunity for her to "horse-trade," to ask for other things in payment for this favor? Perhaps some of the Hazeltyne money that is presumably in the offing?

Other issues: Is there an issue of academic principles involved here? Can Joanna insist on scholarly standards for the library that are more strenuous than those advocated by the president? Is there a role here for the library staff? For the faculty committee on the library? For the university board of trustees? The faculty senate?

41. The Shoemaker's Children Are the Last to Get Shoes (p. 77)

Summary: The manager of the corporate information center has always had strong management support from her boss, but he has retired. She now reports to the director of technology and computer systems, a group from which she has always had strong cooperation. However, that support is now deteriorating. When she mentions this to her new boss, he acknowledges this, but notes that his organization, in order to survive politically, must at least temporarily lessen support to its own units, such as the information center, in order to establish more important priorities.

Questions: Was Marjorie naive in not recognizing that the source of her power had been the personal support of her former boss? How can she develop the same level of support from Charley Horvath? Given his rather frank and direct personality, what sort of strategies might work? Deal making? Promises? Threats? Can she organize information center users and get them to put pressure on Horvath? Should she?

Other issues: Marjorie and Charley clearly have different priorities. Should this surprise Marjorie? How could and should she have anticipated this problem? How could she have prevented it? What does being "a good soldier" mean? Can this be negotiated?

42. The School Library as Detention Center (p. 78)

Summary: New school librarian Melissa Moncrief finds that the library is being used as a place of detention and punishment, apparently with the approval of the principal. This disturbs her because she wants the media center to be perceived by the students as a friendly and useful place.

Questions: Should Melissa have made some sort of attempt to find out about this policy before she took the job? Assuming she had, what if anything should have been her strategy? The use of the library as a detention center is clearly unacceptable, but should she fight this battle now or wait for a more opportune time? Is this the time to take the principal up on her offer to talk to Melissa at any time? What do you think the principal could or would do about this situation? Is this an issue involving the administration, the classroom teachers, or both? Does Melissa really know how widespread this policy of using the library as a detention center is? Is it widespread or is it just Andrea McGinnis's method of handling unruly students? Is it important to find out? How should she find out?

Other issues: What is the larger overriding issue here? Is it the role of the media center in the academic program of the school? If so, how is this problem being addressed at this point? Should Melissa seek out and talk to her predecessor? To other school librarians in the district?

43. The Frills of Public Library On-Line Searching (p. 80)

Summary: Sybil Thornbush has proposed to the board of the public library that the library institute on-line searching for library patrons. The board, led by banker Walter Cunningham, has agreed to fund the hardware and labor costs, but insists that the linear on-line costs be paid for by patrons. Cunningham also rejects the suggestion that the poor be exempted from paying by arguing that the library would have no real basis for making that determination.

Questions: How do you assess Sybil's handling of this discussion, and particularly of board member Cunningham? Are there other persuasive strategies that occur to you? Is the board's willingness to assume hardware and labor costs a fair compromise? Or should Sybil insist on an "all or nothing" approach? Suppose that turns out to be nothing? How significant here are the policies of the ALA and the state library association? How should Sybil explain any deviation to her patrons? To her fellow professionals?

Other issues: This case study is the precursor of case study 14, which deals with staff reactions to the acceptance of this proposed "solution." Does this knowledge now change your assessment in case study 14? In this case, could Sybil have avoided this entire confrontation with the board by approaching the issue differently? Is half a loaf (or some portion of it) better than none? Should Sybil take what she can get now, and hope for more later? Or should she shelve all plans for on-line searching, at least until Cunningham is off the board?

44. A Firing without Recourse (p. 81)

Summary: Virginia Maloney learns that her friend Sandra Mancuso has been fired from her post of public library director, and that the law provides no protection for employees without contracts. Also, Virginia's attempts to deal with this through the state library association are rebuffed because of the concern that this would create conflict between librarians and trustees, who now serve in a joint association and who would probably agree on many things but perhaps not on the rights of library directors in such cases.

Questions: What if anything should Virginia do now? Should she mount a public campaign anyway? Against this particular firing? Against the general lack of protection in the law? Should she bring this matter to the state association anyway? Is it possible that the executive director is wrong, or simply trying to avoid difficulties for herself? Should Virginia sound out other board members informally, including trustee members? Should she talk to her own state representatives? Without the force of law, how likely is the pressure of public suasion going to be in places like Bellfort? Should librarians be warned about working in Bellfort? Should librarians be urged to renegotiate their contracts? Can the state library help here?

Other issues: Is there anything that Sandra Mancuso should have done differently? What are the benefits and drawbacks of the merging of librarian and trustee bodies at the state level? In terms of economy? Of political clout? Of the need for common denominators?

45. One Good Turn May Eventually Earn Another (p. 83)

Summary: Nancy Marlin, librarian at Hermes Insurance, finds that her new supervisor has agreed, without checking with her, to the transfer into the already overcrowded library of five filing cabinets of material. Nancy has previously rejected this transfer. The supervisor says he regrets having done this, but he has already agreed and what is done is done.

Questions: Is this issue only a symptom, and perhaps the first symptom, of Wayne's lack of interest and lack of concern? What can Nancy do to make him care more and be more responsive? Is this the time to seek support from Dr. Rossman and perhaps other library users? Should she make a direct appeal to higher management? Is this a good issue on which to take a stand? Should Nancy seek to enlarge this problem by making this only an example? Or should she try to limit the problem to achieve merely damage control? Is Wayne's action really an accomplished fact or can it be reversed? Should Nancy look at this as an opportunity to get more space? If so, how? What is this favor that Harvey now owes them? Is it real? Is there any way to collect?

Other issues: Librarians almost never have any say in the naming of the individuals who will be their supervisors. What does this suggest in terms of forming larger strategies and programs that are independent of the next supervisor? How could Nancy have prevented the predicament in which she now finds herself? Is it possible that she could not have prevented it?

46. Figure Out a Way to Do More (p. 85)

Summary: Library director Doralynn Smiley has just announced to the assistant director for technical services, Elizabeth Pasternak, that her department's work load would now include the processing of a new and as yet unevaluated and unquantified collection; this would have to be done without additional resources, and the president has committed the library to having all this completed within a year.

Questions: How do you assess the relationship between library director Smiley and the university president? Between Doralynn and her staff? Is there anything that Elizabeth can do to affect, change, or improve that relationship? Should Elizabeth take a firm stand now? Should she first try to assess the amount of work involved? What should she say to her own staff of catalogers? The library director has given the assistant director no specific targets, and has just told her to do the best she can. What does that mean? Trying to work harder? Figuring out a simpler way? Letting the normal backlog grow further? Who takes the blame for this when faculty members complain?

Other issues: Librarians are assumed by some outsiders to have an ability to perform work regardless of resources, and indeed librarians are known to accept such responsibilities. Is that part of the problem here in President Hoagland's actions, or is he treating the library no differently from the rest of the university? In this context, what does Doralynn's statement "I have confidence in you" mean? Is it a compliment? If not, what is it?

47. Programmed for Failure? (p. 86)

Summary: Khalid Morgan, a young black reference librarian, has been offered the post of heading a particularly difficult and troublesome branch of his library. While he wants to be a manager and is initially thrilled at the opportunity, he now has second thoughts that this could be the administration's tactic for getting even with him for having helped maintenance workers in a dispute; he suspects that he is being programmed for failure, and perhaps ultimate dismissal or forced resignation.

Questions: Is Khalid right to be concerned, or is he just imagining things? Should he turn down the promotion? If so, what should he say? How might this affect his chances for future promotion? Should he accept the promotion as a challenge? Should he use the possibility of his acceptance as a bargaining chip to obtain more support for the branch? If so, how should he do this? Are there other people he should talk to before he decides? To whom should he talk, and what should he try to find out?

Other issues: If Khalid asks for more time, asks additional questions, or asks for more support, how is Alex Horowitz, the personnel director, likely to react? Does Khalid need to worry about what that reaction might be? Up to now neither he nor Horowitz has even mentioned his earlier support of the maintenance worker grievance. Should it be kept that way or should he put his suspicions on the table? As the prospective library director in a minority community with which he presumably has some contacts, should he involve his colleagues in the NAACP and the Urban League? To what purpose?

48. The Outraged Professor (p. 89)

Summary: Academic library dean Marjorie Goodlow has received a formal letter from an important new professor from Germany complaining that the chemistry librarian has been rude to him, and he expects an apology from Marjorie and appropriate instruction be given to the librarian. She has had no prior inkling of this case. The chemistry librarian has been forceful and effective, if perhaps slightly abrasive.

Questions: Marjorie certainly needs more information. Should she discuss this letter with Fred (the associate dean for public services) and Monica (the chemistry librarian), or with Monica alone? Should she ask Fred to find out what happened? Do you have any suspicions as to what might have happened? If it turns out that Augenthaler (the professor) tends to treat librarians like clerks, what should Marjorie do? Talk to him? To tell him what?

Talk to the chemistry department chairman? To what purpose? Talk to the president? Apologize to Augenthaler but tell the chemistry librarian to forget it? Or tell her to watch her step? Look for some middle ground, such as a letter of regret that is not a letter of apology about this misunderstanding? Support the chemistry librarian all the way? What is Fred's role in this? The role of other chemistry department faculty?

Other issues: Is there simply a possible personality clash here between a demanding professor with expectations about librarians and an assertive and self-confident librarian? If so, how should this be dealt with? There is a management principle that states "fight for your people if they are right." *If* Monica turns out to be blameless, what does Marjorie owe her? At what risk to the library? Is there perhaps a way of writing something the chemistry professor will accept as an apology but then telling Monica you didn't really mean it and somehow making it up to Monica? Is this a good idea?

49. Education and Ethics (p. 91)

Summary: Public library reference librarian Gwen Martin has reason to suspect that one of the students assigned to read a library book and write a book report may have copied newspaper book reviews instead, although she has no specific proof. The high school teacher who gave the assignment is a good friend of hers.

Questions: Should Gwen alert Pam (the teacher) to her suspicions about Tony? Does she really know that Tony is in Pam's class, working on this assignment? Should she simply alert Pam to the possibility that "a student" might have bypassed this assignment? Is this really any of her business at all? Should she make an effort to talk to Tony, to ascertain why he had proceeded as he had and perhaps to give him a lecture on the importance of education?

Other issues: What are Gwen's responsibilities as a protector of the intellectual rights of her patrons as opposed to her support for the values of education? Does the fact that Tony is a student and not an adult make a difference? What if an adult with a book report to present used the same tactics? Is Gwen's friendship with Pam an issue in this case? Is there concern that by silence she might jeopardize that friendship?

50. A Visit from below the Sea (p. 92)

Summary: The new president at Palmetto State University seeks to upgrade the university academically. As part of this process, and without the knowledge of library director Mary Elizabeth Corrigan, Dr. Corson has been hired to start a new oceanography program starting in a few months. During a visit to Palmetto he asks Mary Elizabeth for the immediate purchase of a substantial number of periodical titles and monographs.

Questions: Should Mary Elizabeth have allowed Dr. Corson to leave without any response from her, which implied that his request would now be met? Should she have told him that she had no prior knowledge of what his meeting with her would be about? Should she argue that she doesn't have the money to fill his request? And is this, in fact, true? What does she need to do now? Buy all the material by reallocating funds? Buy some of the material? Buy none of it then tell Corson later that she had not been involved in the decision? Does she need to talk to President Birnbaum? If so, what should her agenda be? A request for money, or for advance information about projects such as this? A request for a reassessment of library needs and resources based on this new academic agenda? Some combination of these? Anything else?

Other issues: What is your assessment regarding the communications process involving all three people, particularly Mary Elizabeth Corrigan and President Birnbaum? Who is at fault here? Does Mary Elizabeth need to change her agenda and her value system? Can she do this? Should she start looking for another job? How does one impress Birnbaum (and Corson) with the importance of the role of librarians, beyond books and journals? Should Mary Elizabeth contact the librarians at Scripps to find out what to expect? Would this be a breach of confidentiality if done before the announcement of Corson's appointment is made public?

51. One Divided by Two Equals One (p. 95)

Summary: School librarian Harriet Morrison has been told by the assistant superintendent that the departing librarian at the other junior high school in town would not be replaced, and that because of budgetary concerns Harriet would now have to be responsible for both libraries. He also tells her that the staff must take the position in dealing with parents that the quality of their children's education will not be negatively affected by this, which he is certain will be the case. Harriet has just been asked by a prominent parent if this move will indeed occur, and what the impact is likely to be.

Questions: Is Harriet obliged to honor the assistant superintendent's instruction that the teachers and librarians take a positive and optimistic attitude toward this dilution of library service? What are the other teachers, and perhaps the teachers' union, going to do? Does it matter? Should she continue to concentrate on quality service at Grove (her school), recognizing that expectations at Pleasant Ridge (the other junior high) are low? Should she try to equalize the quality of the two school libraries, even at the expense of service at Grove? Is the assistant superintendent's expectation realistic? Is his request fair? What should Harriet tell Doreen, the concerned parent? Should she feign ignorance of proposed changes? Should she tell her she knows but can't discuss the situation? Should she tell Doreen everything? Should she enlist her as an ally for better library service?

Other issues: Should Harriet have said something more to the assistant superintendent? Should she have refused his request? Assured him that quality service to the libraries would suffer and people would notice? Should she have argued for an exemption for library positions, regardless of what else happened? Should she have told him her assessment of library service at Pleasant Ridge and the difference between the library and the one at Grove? Is he aware of any such difference? If the teachers' union has accepted the premise of attrition as the best tactic for achieving cost reductions, can Harriet hope for any help from that source? Is there an inevitable conflict between her loyalty to management and the organization and her loyalty to the school children she wants to serve?

52. When Is a Cost Not a Cost? (p. 96)

Summary: Corporate librarian Heather Freeman has been told, along with other company employees, to accept the reduction of staff through attrition. Her manager's strategy now is to shift the task of literature data-base searching to the actual users. Heather fears that these searches are being done badly or expensively or not being done at all. None of this concerns her boss, who is concentrating only on his own budget.

Questions: Should Heather simply accept this strategy as one that keeps the library out of trouble? Should she make a stronger attempt to point out to Fred (her boss) that this presumed economy is not an economy? Should she try to rally the library users? Should she bypass Fred and try to make her case directly to corporate management, with whom she has some credibility and visibility? What are the risks in this?

Other issues: Do you recognize the similarity in issues between this case study and the previous one, even though one deals with school libraries and one with corporate libraries? The possible conflict between organizational loyalty and professional responsibility is one that applies to just about any profession. Is there a possibility that Heather could have avoided the present problem by the way in which she approached her relationship with Fred?

53. Deselection in the Periodicals Budget (p. 98)

Summary: Academic library director Derek Brownlow has just learned that the renewal of existing serials will involve a cost increase of 19.5 percent, but the university president promises nothing more than 5 percent as a budget increase. His staff opposes shifting other resources to the periodical budgets, and tells him the president must supply additional funds. Brownlow decides instead simply to pass that problem to the academic groups, telling them to submit lists that stay within the 5 percent increase limit.

Questions: How wise was Derek in posing the issue to the professional librarians in this manner? Should he have done so in a different context? Having now reached his decision, should he review this option with the same group? With the university president? The president specified only that this be done in the least traumatic manner. Does this solution qualify? Is there perhaps a better way? How are the faculty departments likely to respond to this decision? If their response is as negative or as emotional as that of his staff, what should he do? What should he do if all cooperate except perhaps one or two? Does he need to be prepared for the possibility of such complaints reaching the president, who might decide that Derek do something other than this and to transfer funds from some other budget?

Other issues: What is your assessment of Derek Brownlow's management style? Of his competence as a manager? Quite aside from the workability of this solution, is it appropriate, or an abdication of responsibility, simply to pass this problem along to the users? Will they pick as carefully and as well as librarians would? You may want to compare your reaction to this case study to that for case study 62.

54. The Use of Volunteers in the School Library (p. 100)

Summary: Superintendent of Schools Hooker has suggested to the supervisor of media services, Florence Galloway, that one possible solution to the problem of continued elimination of school librarian positions through attrition, as forced by budgetary constraints, would be to recruit qualified volunteers to staff school libraries. He reports that the teachers' union would have no objection to such a step, and wants her reaction.

Questions: The use of volunteers in both school and public libraries is a fairly common practice. Do you agree with this approach, do you disagree with it, or do you feel it is acceptable only under certain circumstances? If the last, under what conditions and with what understandings can this be implemented? What sort of conditions for volunteers' work assignments, training, evaluation, and assessment would you suggest? At this point Hooker has not mandated anything. He has asked for Florence's opinion, but he is not planning to replace these librarians, either. What should she say? What are possible alternative suggestions?

Other issues: How could Florence have avoided this issue, if at all? How could she have anticipated it with suggestions of her own? Bear in mind that any proposed approach must be appropriate within the framework of the school system and its budget, as well as the contract and the opinions of the teachers' union.

55. Advice from the Middle School Users (p. 102)

Summary: Greta Lagerquist has established a student advisory committee for her middle school media center. The students take this responsibility and opportunity very seriously, and have made useful and practical suggestions. However, the most recent suggestion concerns the stocking of recreational video games for student use.

Questions: Do you think this is a good suggestion? If you do, how would you move to implement it over potential objection from officials, parents, and taxpayers? If you think it is a bad idea, how should it be dealt with without squelching the enthusiasm of the student committee members? Do you reason and explain, seek to change their minds, or try to manipulate them? Do you pass along their suggestions to the school administration? If so, with what recommendations, if any?

Other issues: If an advisory committee is established, one must be prepared for all kinds of advice. Is there any way Greta could or should have forestalled this, perhaps by giving the committee more specific ground rules? If there a major problem at this point? Could one develop if she is not careful? In what direction or directions? There is always the option of turning down this suggestion by stating that the principal would never approve it. What do you think of such a strategy?

56. A Problem with Vandalism (p. 103)

Summary: School librarian Paula Kenton, who has accepted customarily low levels of theft of library materials as a fairly normal cost of operations, is concerned at the high rate of thefts of CD/ROM discs, which can be very expensive. Since she assumes that these have no practical use for the thieves, she attributes the matter to vandalism, and wonders what to do.

Questions: Is Paula correct in her assumption that this is simple vandalism, with no other motivation for the thefts? Does she need to take an inventory and quantify the problem before she proceeds further? Assuming she finds that theft is commonplace and not just occasional, what are her options? Stopping the purchase of discs? Tighter security procedures? What kind? Discussing the matter with school administrators, who are currently unaware of the problem? Should she simply shrug off the losses but put the discs under tighter security to prevent recurrence?

Other issues: Could or should this problem have been anticipated? Prevented through better procedures? How does one maintain a balance between tighter security and the appearance of a police environment that signifies distrust of the students?

57. Helping Love Along (p. 104)

Summary: The director of an aerospace company's technical information center receives a written request from Christine Andrews, a shipping clerk for the company that distributes a British technical journal, to show her letter and picture to any single young engineers who might be interested in starting a correspondence.

Questions: Should Neil (the director) simply throw the letter and picture away? Should he return the picture to Chris, pointing out that he can't comply with her request? Should he write to the journal editor to complain? Should he pass the correspondence and photograph along to certain engineers he knows to be single? Should he simply post the letter on the bulletin board for anyone who might like to respond?

Other issues: This case study might appear farfetched, but it is very real. It is at present not a very serious issue; indeed, not all problems are. However, could it become a problem? Or does it simply provide an opportunity for some human interest publicity for the library?

58. This Is the Year for Chaucer (p. 105)

Summary: A community college professor has made what appears to be a totally unreasonable demand for the purchase of Chaucer literature, a considerable addition to the collection that the college and the library clearly do not need. The department chairman agrees with the unreasonableness of the request, but asks that at least some of the material be purchased to help assuage the disappointment of a professor who has begun to realize that his options for moving to a higher-level institution are fading. The chairman asks for this action to help salvage the professor's dignity.

Questions: How reasonable do you consider Chairman Rappoport's request? Should Salvatore Callini, the library director, accede to it or simply refuse Professor Goodnight? Should Sal expect Rappoport to pass on the bad news to Goodnight, or tell him himself? What might happen next? Is this an investment in Rappoport's good will, and is it worth it? Should Sal go over Rappoport's head to the dean of the College of Arts or to some other administrator?

Other issues: What is the library's role in assuaging the egos of faculty members as compared to an antiseptic process of collection evaluation? Is it possible that some of this happens anyway in faculty recommendation, even if perhaps not as blatantly? Is there an issue of library autonomy here that must be fought? Of intellectual freedom as represented in selection policy?

59. I Want My Favorite Reference Librarian (p. 108)

Summary: The public library has a policy of rotating the assignments of reference librarians to telephone reference service. The head of reference reports at a staff meeting that some patrons demand to be served by specific reference librarians rather than simply by whoever answers the phone.

Questions: Should Hubbell (the head of reference) have brought this up at the staff meeting, in a private meeting, or perhaps not at all? Are the users justified in demanding service from specific reference librarians, or are they being unreasonable? If the library tries to accommodate this request, how will it affect workload assignments and scheduling? Might it have a negative effect on library cost and efficiency?

Other issues: If you think the users are being unreasonable, how do *you* feel about being served by any next available barber or hair stylist, or even bank teller? Should Ernestina (the library director) make an attempt to find out which reference librarians are in heavy demand and why? Should this be a factor in performance evaluation and salary increases? By contrast, if some reference librarians are being avoided, does Ernestina need to know who these people are and why? Do you have any assessment of Malcolm Hubbell as a manager?

60. To Serve the Will of God (p. 109)

Summary: Albert Millgran, the newly arrived public library director, receives a letter from the minister of a large fundamentalist church inviting him to visit and join the church. It also suggests a meeting, so that the two can discuss ways to "further God's work" effectively.

Questions: Is Millgran correct in his assumption that this letter means trouble? Is it possible that it has no specific meaning, and that the closing ("Yours in Christ") simply represents a style of writing? Does the secretary's classifying this as routine mean anything—about the importance of the letter or the competence of the secretary? If the minister, Kingford, signifies the potential for trouble, wouldn't the library's assistant director and board of trustees know? Should you ask them before responding to this invitation?

Other issues: Can Millgran simply ignore the letter, or must he respond? Can he beg off from a meeting, indicating that he is very busy, or should he meet with the minister? Would lunch be a good setting, or is there a preferable one? Is this the time to brush up on issues of intellectual freedom, censorship, and ALA guidelines and policies?

61. I Don't Want My Child to Bring Home Dirty Books (p. 110)

Summary: Mrs. Lindstrom is upset at library materials selected by her ten-year-old daughter and demands that the library staff monitor what the child charges out of the library. Told that the library has no such procedures, she storms out of the building, threatening to forbid her daughter to use the library.

Questions: Did Edna Mulloy, the library director, handle this situation as well as she could have? Was there any reasonable ground for further discussion to keep Mrs. Lindstrom from storming out of the library? What should Edna do now? Anything or nothing at all? If Jennifer Lindstrom reappears in the library, should she be asked if she is violating her mother's instructions? Mrs. Lindstrom's further threats are vague, but should Edna alert anyone else? The staff? The board? The library's legal counsel or the city attorney?

Other issues: Does the library have a clearly stated written policy to cover this kind of situation? What happens if there is really no official policy, if the library is simply using what it considers common sense and following general accepted professional library procedures? If Mrs. Lindstrom asks that her daughter be restricted to borrowing material from the children's collection (or barred from access to the adult room), can the library assume either or both of these obligations? *Should* it? If, as a result of this, Jennifer fails to reappear at the library, would you feel guilty? Would you then contact Mrs. Lindstrom or let it go?

62. Periodical Cancellations during Tough Times (p. 111)

Summary: The university's library director faces a budget that will not allow the renewal of periodical subscriptions. The faculty suggest protecting the periodicals budget by delaying automation and reducing staff through attrition and the librarians are unable to agree on a strategy. Warren Hobson, the library director, decides to let the net periodicals budget grow by only 4 percent, and instructs each budget manager to accomplish this.

Questions: How do you assess Warren's tactics so far? Has he done everything he could have done, or are there additional options? What does the silence of the staff suggest—agreement or hopeless confusion? Do you agree with his protection of automation and of staff positions and salaries? Will the staff be able to implement Warren's aims and how will users react? Is this staff assignment fair and balanced, or unfair and arbitrary?

Other issues: Compare this case study to case study 53, in which the budget-cutting assignment is given directly to the faculty instead of to the staff. Assess the political implications, the likelihood of better decisions under these alternatives, and possible other options.